"Understanding the past has never been so necessary. Robert Gildea tells us why and shows us how it can be done better. An indispensable book for us all."
Joanna Bourke,
Birkbeck, University of London

"A clear-eyed and necessary approach to why understanding the past is crucial in the present. Robert Gildea argues the importance of history, in navigating major movements and issues we face today, from de-colonisation to fake news. But, crucially, Gildea charts the undulations of history as a discipline, clearly and thoughtfully demonstrating exactly why history must always be re-written. This book should be planted firmly in the hands of every history student."
Helen Carr,
Queen Mary University of London

"This book stuns. With clarity, with energy, with brilliance, Gildea reveals what is at stake in the many battles about history. He explains why history is evoked whenever regimes change or wars are fought. The book could hardly be more timely."
Joya Chatterji,
University of Cambridge

The status quo is broken. Humanity today faces multiple interconnected challenges, some of which could prove existential. If we believe the world could be different, if we want it to be *better*, examining the purpose of what we do – and what is done in our name – is more pressing than ever.

The What Is It For? series examines the purpose of the most important aspects of our contemporary world, from religion and free speech to animal rights and the Olympics. It illuminates what these things are by looking closely at what they do.

The series offers fresh thinking on current debates that gets beyond the overheated polemics and easy polarizations. Across the series, leading experts explore new ways forward, enabling readers to engage with the possibility of real change.

Series editor: George Miller

Visit **bristoluniversitypress.co.uk/what-is-it-for** to find out more about the series.

Available now

WHAT **ARE ANIMAL RIGHTS FOR?**
Steve Cooke

WHAT **IS CYBERSECURITY FOR?**
Tim Stevens

WHAT **IS HISTORY FOR?**
Robert Gildea

WHAT **IS PHILANTHROPY FOR?**
Rhodri Davies

WHAT **IS WAR FOR?**
Jack McDonald

Forthcoming

WHAT **IS ANTHROPOLOGY FOR?**
Kriti Kapila

WHAT **IS COUNTERTERRORISM FOR?**
Leonie Jackson

WHAT **IS DRUG POLICY FOR?**
Julia Buxton

WHAT **IS FREE SPEECH FOR?**
Gavan Titley

WHAT **IS HUMANISM FOR?**
Richard Norman

WHAT IS IMMIGRATION POLICY FOR?
Madeleine Sumption

WHAT IS JOURNALISM FOR?
Jon Allsop

WHAT IS THE MONARCHY FOR?
Laura Clancy

WHAT ARE MUSEUMS FOR?
Jon Sleigh

WHAT IS MUSIC FOR?
Fleur Brouwer

WHAT ARE NUCLEAR WEAPONS FOR?
Patricia Shamai

WHAT ARE PRISONS FOR?
Hindpal Singh Bhui

WHAT IS RELIGION FOR?
Malise Ruthven

WHAT ARE STATUES FOR?
Milly Williamson

WHAT ARE THE OLYMPICS FOR?
Jules Boykoff

WHAT IS VEGANISM FOR?
Catherine Oliver

WHAT ARE ZOOS FOR?
Heather Browning and Walter Veit

ROBERT GILDEA is Professor Emeritus of modern history at the University of Oxford. His publications include *Barricades and Borders: Europe 1800–1914* (Short Oxford History of the Modern World), *Empires of the Mind: The Colonial Past and the Politics of the Present*, the Wolfson Prize-winning *Marianne in Chains: In Search of the German Occupation 1940–45*, and *Backbone of the Nation: Mining Communities and the Great Strike of 1984–85*.

WHAT IS HISTORY FOR?

ROBERT GILDEA

First published in Great Britain in 2024 by

Bristol University Press
University of Bristol
1–9 Old Park Hill
Bristol
BS2 8BB
UK
t: +44 (0)117 374 6645
e: bup-info@bristol.ac.uk

Details of international sales and distribution partners are available at
bristoluniversitypress.co.uk

British Library Cataloguing in Publication Data
A catalogue record for this book is available from the British Library

ISBN 978-1-5292-3051-2 paperback
ISBN 978-1-5292-3052-9 ePub
ISBN 978-1-5292-3053-6 ePdf

Cover design: Tom Appshaw

To my former students,
and students of history everywhere

CONTENTS

List of Figures and Boxes — **xiii**

Preface: Snails in the Tank — **xv**

1 **Where Are We Now?** — **1**

Myth-making and myth-busting — 1

Controlling the narrative — 6

History and identity — 13

2 **How Did We Get Here?** — **18**

Appealing to the mythical past — 18

Historians and myth — 30

History and power: the struggle for legitimacy — 54

Whose history is it anyway? History and identity — 88

3   **Where Do We Go From Here?**   **122**

   Working through   122

   Who writes history?   133

Notes   **140**

Further Reading   **153**

Index   **158**

LIST OF FIGURES AND BOXES

Figures

1.1 Statue of St Vladimir, Moscow (Creative Commons Attribution 4.0 International) 5

2.1 *Homecoming of the Militiaman from the War of Liberation*, oil painting by Johann Peter Krafft, 1817 (Belvedere, Vienna. Reproduced under Attribution-Share Alike 4.0 International License, CC BY-SA 4.0) 22

2.2 *From the Cape to Cairo* by Udo Keppler, cartoon from *Puck* magazine, 1902 (Library of Congress, public domain) 26

2.3 *Assassination of Julius Caesar*, drawing by Vincenzo Camuccini, 1793–96 (Metropolitan Museum of Art, New York, public domain) 58

2.4 The Declaration of Independence, first printed version, produced by John Dunlap, 1776 (World Digital Library) 62

2.5 From *Scenes on a Cotton Plantation*, sketched by A.R. Waud (*Harper's Weekly*, 1867), wood engraving (detail) (Library of Congress, public domain) 72

2.6 'Struggle session' at Tsinghua University High School, May 1966 (unidentified photographer) 85

2.7 Fighting in Père Lachaise cemetery, Paris, 1871   93
(from *Mémorial Illustré des Deux Sièges de
Paris, 1870–1871*) (Bibliothèque patrimoniale
des Archives de Paris, 1Gb 164, Open Licence)

2.8 A suffragette arrested in the street in London,   102
1914 (Gallica, Bibliothèque nationale de France,
Agence Rol 39114, public domain)

3.1 Black Lives Matter rally, H Street,   127
Washington, DC, 4 June 2020, photographed
by Tracy Meehleib (Library of Congress, Prints
& Photographs Division, © Tracy Meehleib,
[LC-DIG-ppbd-01157], reproduced by
permission of the photographer)

Boxes

1.1 Russian national identity   7
1.2 *Our Island Story*   10
1.3 Are statues history?   14
2.1 The historical novel   34
2.2 Whig history   37
2.3 Merrie England   40
2.4 Revisionism   44
2.5 Historical frames or lenses   49
2.6 The Old South   70
2.7 Marxist history   79
2.8 The Chinese Cultural Revolution   84
2.9 The Paris Commune   92
2.10 Why dates matter   119

PREFACE: SNAILS IN THE TANK

1960s. When I was at school, thinking about what I might do later in life, my father told me I should become a civil servant, like him. He was working at the Board of Trade, involved in the UK's second attempt to join the Common Market. I was passionate about history – at that time that of the English Civil War – and needed an argument to persuade my father than the civil service was not for me. Since I kept newts and put snails into their tank to purify the water, it occurred to me that historians were like snails in the water tank of societies, cleaning up the misconceptions they had about their past and helping them to see more clearly. Although I would not yet have used the term, I was feeling my way towards the idea that historians were critical of received opinions. Later I discovered French history, and my doctoral research engaged with what I thought was a misconception about French centralization. The story ran that an education minister of Napoleon III in the 1860s boasted that he could look at his watch and tell what subject every schoolchild in France was studying at that moment. I decided to put this to the test and wrote a thesis on education in the distant province of Brittany, to see whether the myth stood up to evidence from the archives.

1980s. After I got my first academic job, I was asked to write a survey on nineteenth-century Europe for the Short Oxford History of the Modern World. *Barricades and Borders* covered not only revolution and nationalism but economic, social and cultural change. When it came out, I was challenged by an American historian who had written a book on women workers in northern France in that period. 'You write about industrial workers as if they were all men', she said. 'Don't you know that the vast majority of textile workers were women?' To my shame I realized that I had been insensitive to gender and failed to integrate the histories of women that were now being published downstream of second-wave feminism. From this point I became attentive to looking at history not only through the lens of class but also through that of gender.

2010s. In time I came to see that history also had to be understood through the lens of race. While writing a book on the French Resistance in the Second World War, I was shocked by the fact that the same resisters who had liberated France from its North African possessions in 1944 were back in Algeria ten years later torturing Algerians who were fighting for their own freedom. Invited to deliver a series of lectures in Belfast in 2013, I took the theme of the difficulties the French had casting off their colonial past, whether that took the form of thinking that they still ruled Africa or of treating immigrants of African origin as second-class citizens. Then Brexit happened, and I decided that I also had to find out about Britain's attitude to its colonial past. It became clear to me that Brexit was based on a fantasy that the British Empire would be reborn once the country left the European Union, and for the first time I wrote a book with political intention. In my naivety, I thought that *Empires of the Mind* would stop Brexit. I could not have been more wrong. The book had almost no coverage. What little it did have was not complimentary. This was not a story that anyone wanted to hear. Global Britain may have been a fantasy, but it was a fantasy that people liked. I realized that myth was more seductive than history, however hard this proposition is for historians to swallow.

This book seeks to answer the question: what is history for? This is by no means an easy question. Historians are familiar with the question, 'what is history?'; what it is for, much less so. For this suggests that history is not simply an academic subject, to be studied for its own sake. It has a social function, a political function. It may make help us to live better lives or to govern ourselves better. Or it may make things worse. There is good history, and there is bad history.

The first chapter of the book asks the question from the viewpoint of the contemporary world. It uses recent events to show how both governors and the governed use history to justify the expansion of their empires, to legitimate the power that they hold or to make claims based on their identity.

The second chapter of the book explores how we reached where we are now. Here historians are on safer ground. We explore the differences between history and myth and discuss the famous injunction of the nineteenth century that the task of historians was only to 'show what actually happened'. We then move on to how history is used to legitimate political power within states. Monarchs claim to rule on the basis of heredity, and sometimes on that of a god-given right. Such claims may be challenged by democracies, which claim legitimacy from successful revolution, and embody a revolutionary tradition. The third part of the chapter examines how history is invoked by groups who feel excluded from the mainstream history, which is so often written by and about middle-class white men. These groups are increasingly writing their own history in order to define their identity and make claims on the basis of their difference.

The final chapter of the book offers some thoughts about where we go from here. Historians are now on treacherous ground, because they cannot predict the future. What we can do, however, is suggest how societies need to 'work through' painful and even traumatic moments of their past and to insist that history-writing is far too important to be left to academic historians.

Robert Gildea
Oxford, November 2023

1
WHERE ARE WE NOW?

Myth-making and myth-busting

In an article written in July 2021, six months before his troops invaded Ukraine, Russian president Vladimir Putin argued that Russians and Ukrainians were united by a common history, a common faith, a common civilization and a common blood. This, he said, could be traced back to the medieval state of Kyivan Rus':

> I am confident that true sovereignty of Ukraine is possible only in partnership with Russia. Our spiritual, human and civilizational ties formed for centuries have their origins in the same sources, they have been hardened by common trials, achievements and victories. Our kinship has been transmitted from generation to generation. It is in the hearts and the memory of people living in modern Russia and Ukraine, in the blood ties that unite millions of our families. Together we have always been and will be many times stronger and more successful. For we are one people.[1]

He blamed the Communist regime for having created the Soviet Union as a federal state in 1922, a 'time bomb' which resulted in the independence of Ukraine after the collapse of the Soviet Union in 1989–91. Ukrainian leaders, according to Putin, then turned against their Russian brothers and demonized them:

> They began to mythologize and rewrite history, edit out everything that united us, and refer to the period when Ukraine was part of the Russian Empire and the Soviet Union as an occupation. The common tragedy of collectivization and famine of the early 1930s was portrayed as the genocide of the Ukrainian people.[2]

Putin reiterated this case in a speech on 21 February 2022, the day before his invasion. He accused Ukraine not only of turning against Mother Russia but of siding with the West. It had made a 'so-called pro-Western civilizational choice' which had allowed the North Atlantic Treaty Organization (NATO) to 'reach Russia's borders … like a knife to the throat'.[3]

The following day United States president Joe Biden accused Putin of a 'twisted rewrite of history'. A month later, at the royal castle in Warsaw, Biden proposed a version of Russian history in which the Soviet regime from 1956 to 1989 and Putin's Russia shared a common desire to dominate neighbouring states. The US, meanwhile, he declared, resisted this aggression during the Cold War and emerged as the leader of the free world, a responsibility that it was not going to give up:

Today's fighting in Kyiv and Mariupol and Kharkiv are the latest battle in a long struggle: Hungary, 1956; Poland, 1956 then again 1981; Czechoslovakia, 1968.

Soviet tanks crushed democratic uprisings, but the resistance continued until finally, in 1989, the Berlin Wall and all of the walls of Soviet domination — they fell. They fell. And the people prevailed. ... But we emerged anew in the great battle for freedom: a battle between democracy and autocracy, between liberty and repression, between a rules-based order and one governed by brute force.[4]

The 'we' for Biden bound together a number of circles of freedom lovers. First, since he was in Warsaw, he paid homage to the Poles who had freed themselves from Soviet domination 30 years before under the leadership of the Solidarity trade union and Pope John Paul II. Second, there were the Ukrainians, who were now the advance guard of the fight for freedom and independence. Finally, there were the democracies of the West that Putin had been unable to divide and which were now rallying to the military, economic and humanitarian assistance of their Ukrainian friends.

In these speeches both political leaders used history to defend their claims to exercise power in the international sphere. The history of empires and nations has repeatedly been invoked to justify their claims. But that history has generally been less history than myth. By myth we mean not a fiction, which has no truth in it, but a narrative that serves a political purpose. That political purpose is to define a political community, to bind it together and to legitimate its aims both to itself and to others. The myth would demonstrate that they were right and their enemies were wrong. For Putin, the political community was that of a Russia that for many centuries had included Ukraine and was ranged against a West which it saw as a constant threat to its existence. For Biden, the purpose was to bring together Western Europe, the former Eastern bloc and the United States by demonstrating their historic commitment against Soviet and Russian despotism in defence of the 'free world'.

We could, of course, take these speeches at face value. There is truth in them, but the truths have been selected to spin myths that begin to part company from the truth. The task of historians is to study these narratives with a critical eye. They analyse the language that is being used, by whom and why. They place the speakers back in their historical context, try to account for the history they were making use of and explain what they were trying to achieve. Shaun Walker, for example, points out that in 1989 Putin was a KGB lieutenant colonel in East Germany, where communism was collapsing. Putin later said, 'I had the feeling that the country was no more. It had disappeared.' Two years later the Soviet Union, which had been formed after the Bolshevik Revolution of 1917, itself collapsed, and with it, its de facto empire in Eastern Europe, the Baltics and Ukraine. In 2005, five years into his presidency, he declared that this collapse was 'the greatest geopolitical catastrophe of the twentieth century'. Putin mobilized history to claim that, from his annexation of Crimea in 2014, he had embarked on a project of restoring

Russia's past greatness. Walker highlights his unveiling outside the Kremlin in 2016 of a 17-metre-high statue of his namesake Vladimir the Great, grand prince of Kyiv and ruler of Kyivan Rus' (980–1015), while the patriarch of the Orthodox Church declared that 'without Vladimir there would have been no Rus', no Russia, no Russian Orthodox church, no great Russian Empire and no modern Russia'.[5]

Further explanation was provided by historian Timothy Snyder. He underlined how threatened Putin felt by the expansion of the European Union (EU) and NATO between 1997 and 2007 to include central and eastern European countries and the three Baltic states,

Figure 1.1: Statue of St Vladimir, Moscow

This statue of St Vladimir, ruler of Kyivan Rus', was unveiled opposite the Kremlin in 2016. Statues are often used to construct myths, here that the Russia of his namesake, Vladimir Putin, had a historic claim to Ukraine.

which had only recently been part of the Communist bloc, and by the pro-EU protests in Kyiv in 2014 which provoked Putin's annexation of the Crimea. Snyder also pointed out that the United States had not defended the free world consistently since the Second World War, and that President Trump had retreated into isolationism, praised the populism and nationalist nostalgia of Putin and may well have been helped into power by the Kremlin.[6] Other historians have broadened the context still further, showing how there are really two Americas: one that harks back to the 1776 Declaration of Independence and poses as the leader of the free world; the other, characterized by the Central Intelligence Agency (CIA), which has systematically put down movements, and even regimes, from the Middle East and Asia to Africa and Latin America which the US has regarded as threatening its national security and strategic interests.[7]

Controlling the narrative

In May 2014 President Putin had a law passed which criminalized the 'public distribution of lies about the activities of the Soviet Union in World War II'. Victory in what Russians call the Great Patriotic War against Hitler was another building block of Russian greatness and it was forbidden to mention embarrassing facts such as Stalin's pact with Hitler in 1939 or the mass deportation of minority ethnic groups during the war.[8] Then in July 2021 he set up a commission of historical education in order to ensure a unified approach to teaching the history of the Russian Federation and to combat attempts to 'falsify history'. 'Like any country, the government is trying to preserve the state', said official historian Pavel Pozhigailo, and then warned, 'If history is rewritten, the state will no longer exist.'[9]

1.1: Russian national identity

In his first 'philosophical letter', written in 1836, Peter Chaadayev, a veteran of the war of 1812, wrote that Russia did not have an identity: 'Not one useful thought has germinated on the barren soil of our country, not one great thought has sprung up in our midst.' The Tsarist regime declared him insane, but he stimulated a debate between Westernizers, who said that Russia had been modernized by Peter the Great and was part of the Enlightened West, and Slavophiles, who argued that Russia was different, characterized by the Orthodox Church, the peasant commune and traditional Zemsky Sobor (parliament of nobles, officials, clergy and merchants). Russian revolutionaries in the nineteenth century were Westernizers, but the Tsar held that Russia was defined by autocracy, orthodoxy and nationality. The Russian Revolution of 1917 embraced Western democracy and then Marxism, but Stalin distanced himself from the West, prioritizing 'Socialism in One Country' and commemorating the Great Patriotic War. The Putin regime returned to the Russia of autocracy, orthodoxy and nationality and attempted to smother West-facing Ukraine.

In 2018, meanwhile, President Xi Jinping of the People's Republic of China denounced what he called 'historical nihilism'. This, he said, 'distorts modern Chinese revolutionary history, the history of the Communist Party and the history of the People's Republic. The crucial point of historical nihilism is to fundamentally negate the leading position of Marxism, the inevitability that China would take the socialist path, and the leadership of the CCP [Chinese Communist Party].'[10]

What both these examples suggest is that rulers, especially but not exclusively in dictatorships, are keen to keep control of what history is taught and to authorize only those interpretations that defend their regime as sanctioned by history. These interpretations generally have three elements. First, that the history of their country or empire is exceptional. Second, that this history is continuous, a straight line between past and present. And third, that this history is teleological, that it points towards a future of happiness and strength. Inevitably, they have to smooth over or suppress alternative interpretations which point to conflict, discontinuity and contingency. In the case of Russia, victory in the Great Patriotic War glossed over the fact that both the Russian Empire and the Soviet Union had collapsed ignominiously and that it had modernized only by the brutality of Stalinism. In the case of China, the rise of the Chinese Communist Party after 1949 came after a 'century of humiliation' by Western powers and Japan between the Opium Wars of the mid-nineteenth century and the Second World War. Moreover, China too had modernized only through the authoritarianism of its Communist Party. Economic progress was not accompanied by political democracy. Indeed, the brutal suppression of pro-democracy protesters in Tiananmen Square in the spring of 1989 remained unmentionable in accounts of Chinese history. Xi Jinping sought to overcome these contradictions by appealing to history in order to promote Chinese nationalism. China was now asserting itself economically and militarily, becoming a global power through the Belt and Road Initiative by sea via the Indian Ocean and by land along the old Silk Road, and becoming the world's second military power after the United States.[11]

It may be imagined that such efforts to control the writing of history to ensure the survival of the state have been confined to dictatorships. But even in democracies, ruling parties seek to control the historical narrative in order to defend the established regime. When the Conservative Party returned to power in 2010, education secretary Michael Gove insisted that history teaching in Britain foregrounded a continuous British national story of sovereignty and empire. 'The current approach we have to history denies children the opportunity to hear our island story', he told the Conservative Party Conference that autumn. 'Children are given a cursory run through Henry VIII and Hitler without knowing how the vivid episodes of our past become a connected narrative. Well, this trashing of our past has to stop.'[12] Central to that story was the thousand-year rule of the British monarchy, reinforced by the 70-year reign of Queen Elizabeth II (1952–2022). When she died and a few republicans protested in the streets, the state hit back with considerable force. When, at a ceremony in Edinburgh proclaiming the new king, a student, Mariángela, held up a placard that read, 'Fuck Imperialism. Abolish the Monarchy', she was promptly arrested. The government rushed through a public order Bill to give the government additional powers to silence peaceful protest, and at the coronation of Charles III on 6 May 2023 fifty demonstrators who waved placards reading 'Abolish the Monarchy' and 'Not my King' were also arrested.

1.2: *Our Island Story*

Our Island Story. A Child's History of England was published by Scottish writer Henrietta Elizabeth Marshall in 1905. It told the story of the growth of English freedom in struggles against the Romans, the Normans, bad kings, the Spaniards and the French, and of the expansion of England, bringing freedom and civilization to benighted parts of the world. It was satirized by Oxford-educated schoolmasters W.C. Sellar and R.J. Yeatman in *1066 and All That* (1930) – which divided history into 'Good Things' and 'Bad Things' – but drew on conventional Whig history and became a standard narrative replicated by authors such as Arthur Bryant, A.L. Rowse, R.J. Unstead and Winston Churchill in his *History of the English-Speaking Peoples*. The English exceptionalism of the story was weaponized by anti-Europeans and criticized by those who argued that it excluded the experiences of people of colour.

Historian David Cannadine has shown that the modern tradition of the monarchy was literally invented after Victoria became Empress of India in 1877, and was further boosted by her jubilees in 1887 and 1897. Elaborately choreographed ceremony, which accentuated consensus, stability and continuity but used commercialism, the mass media and later social media, secured mass support as an antidote to a rapidly changing and uncertain world.[13] And yet the history of the British monarchy was not continuous. It was abolished between 1649 and 1660, shaken by the French Revolution and discredited by the abdication of Edward VIII in 1936, when protesters waved placards reading 'Abdication means Revolution'.

Despite the myth-making, history has never continued in a straight line, not least because political regimes have constantly been overthrown and replaced, destroyed and recreated. Historical accounts have to wrestle not only with lack of continuity but with the changing source of legitimacy. In theory, state power, of course, might be exercised by brute force. But to survive it needs to be accompanied by authority. Rulers had to demonstrate that they had authority either from above, bestowed by God, which generally required the sanction of church leaders, or from below, delegated by popular sovereignty through election. In both cases history was mobilized. Kingly rule might be traced back along a hereditary line to the founder of a dynasty. Democratic rule might be traced back to a revolution that overthrew a tyrant or tyrannical regime.

When power was contested, so too was history. Those who overthrew rulers by denouncing them as tyrants justified what they did by reference to the overthrow of other tyrants or those who aspired to tyranny, as in the case of the assassination of Julius Caesar in 44 BCE. New rulers justified themselves by not being tyrants and modelling themselves on good kings or emperors who had gone before. In the modern era, however, monarchical regimes as such have been overthrown. This posed a problem for the historical account. For a long while modern republican regimes presented themselves as new versions of the Roman republic that had existed between the overthrow of their tyrants and the return of emperors. In time, however, and once a revolution had succeeded, the revolution itself – the founding of a new order – became the source of legitimacy. The American Revolution of 1776, the French Revolution of 1789, the Russian Revolution of 1917 and the Chinese Revolution of 1949 became the sacred founding moments of subsequent revolutionary regimes. A new problem nevertheless arose. Because revolutions were born from violence, new violence might be justified. So how could regimes that emerged from revolution justify themselves by reference to history? Thinking about the Russian Revolution and publishing *Nineteen Eighty-Four* in the same year as the Chinese Revolution, George Orwell imagined what the party that controlled a communist state would say. It went for communist states, but it also had meaning for liberal, non-communist states, which were perhaps not quite as liberal as they made out: 'Who controls the past controls the future: who controls the present controls the past.'[14]

History and identity

On 25 May 2020 forty-six-year-old George Floyd was arrested, tortured and killed by Minneapolis police officers. The minutes it took him to die with a policeman's knee on his neck were captured on film and disseminated by social media across the world. The outrage was taken up by Black Lives Matter, a movement founded in 2013 to protest against police racism and police violence.

The moment was seized on across the world to deface or topple monuments, often statues, that were seen to honour white supremacy, enslavement and colonialism. These statues were often erected years after the death of the individual they commemorated, and their place was now contested by protesters. On 10 June 2020 protesters in Richmond, Virginia, pulled down the statue of Jefferson Davis, the president of the Confederate States that fought to preserve slavery in America's Civil War, which had been unveiled in 1907. In Washington an equestrian statue of President Andrew Jackson, the populist president responsible for the forcible removal of Native Americans west of the Mississippi in the 1830s in what became known as the 'Trail of Tears', was overturned. In Belgium statues in Antwerp and Ghent to King Leopold II, whose brutal colonization of the Congo led to millions of deaths, were defaced and later removed. In Britain a statue of Bristol-born slave trader Edward Colston was toppled by a crowd and tipped into Bristol harbour on 7 June 2020. On 16 June that year students in Oxford marched to demand the removal from the walls of Oriel College of the statue of the white supremacist and imperialist Cecil Rhodes that overlooks the High Street.

1.3: Are statues history?

Statues embody the collective memory that commemorates (remembers in common) historical figures or events. They are raised by public authorities to pay homage to national heroes or victims. They use those who have gone before to impart some lesson to the political community. They are thus part of the legitimizing work of history.

Controversy often arises when statues are defaced or pulled down. This happens at moments of revolution, regime change or sudden changes of historical context, such as the emergence of the Black Lives Matter movement. An opportunity arises for people to dismantle the statues of kings, generals or benefactors which have long insulted or humiliated them. Others feel that the same statues should still be honoured and defended from 'vandals'. In the case of war or Holocaust memorials, attempts to desecrate them have been met by general condemnation.

Later in the summer of 2020 Britain was racked by a controversy about whether 'Rule Britannia' should be played by the BBC at the Last Night of the Proms. Composed in 1740 and reflecting Britain's rise as a colonial power, it acquired the status of an alternative national anthem. Musician Chi-chi Nwanoku, herself of mixed Nigerian and Irish heritage and speaking for the majority Black and ethnically diverse Chineke! Orchestra, protested that the anthem amplified 'jingoistic echoes of empire' and that the sentiment that 'Britons shall never be slaves … implies that it's OK for others to be slaves but not us'. The BBC considered a plan to play the anthem in an orchestral version but then government ministers became involved. On 25 August prime minister Boris Johnson proclaimed, 'I think it's time we stopped our cringing embarrassment about our history, about our traditions, and about our culture, and we stopped this general fight of self-recrimination and wetness.'[15] In the end, tradition prevailed and 'Rule Britannia' was played as usual for another year.

What was contested here was identity. Or rather identities. On the one hand, the identity of a dominant white American or British nation that was keen to silence the voices and marginalize the identity of formerly enslaved Black populations. On the other, representatives of those populations who challenged a view of history that they felt was a distortion and fought to define their identity and recover a voice. Both appealed to history. The protesters were keen to pull down the statues and edit the anthems that honoured those who promoted slavery, colonialism and white supremacy. Their opponents defended those statues and anthems on the grounds that 'you can't rewrite history'. This meant, fairly sensibly, that you can't deny the events that actually happened in the past. But it also encouraged people to believe that the history in the history books could not be rewritten. What they were really saying was: 'You should not rewrite the history that we have already written.'

And yet history *was* being rewritten in order to accommodate the experience of Black populations. Catherine Hall argued in 2014 that 'slave-ownership was virtually invisible in British history' before her project of 2009–12 analysing it from the records of those slave owners who were compensated after the abolition of slavery in British colonies in 1834. She and her team demonstrated that slave ownership and compensation payments underpinned much of the wealth of the Victorian aristocracy, gentry and middle class, even as they congratulated themselves as architects of the 'Age of Reform'.[16] Historian David Olusoga, Nigerian-born and brought up in Gateshead, felt 'profoundly unwelcome in Britain' and was driven out of the family home in 1984 by a National Front attack. The way he became 'of Britain' was to 'reclaim [the] lost past' of the black population of Britain, the first of whom were the Africans who came over as part of the Roman army.[17]

Defenders of 'our island story', however, were not going to let such historical revisionism gain a foothold as the accepted narrative. In his 2023 *Colonialism*, Nigel Biggar, Professor Emeritus of Moral and Pastoral Theology at the University of Oxford, emphasized that slavery was ancient and universal, not only confined to the Atlantic slave trade, and that the Christian and humanitarian campaign to abolish the slave trade between 1787 and 1807 more properly defined the British. 'The British Empire', he continued, 'was not essentially racist', while 'the report of the British government's Commission on Race and Ethnic Disparities, which was published in March 2021, argued that contemporary Britain is not in fact structurally racist'.[18]

Meanwhile, in the United States, Donald Trump's attempts by political and legal machinations to reverse the 2020 presidential election that deprived him of power were disproportionately targeted on cities such as Detroit, Philadelphia and Atlanta, which have large Black populations. For many civil rights groups this smacked of regular attempts to prevent African Americans voting, which could be traced back to post-Civil War segregation and intimidation.[19] Even more extraordinary, some Trump supporters defended the 6 January 2021 assault on the Capitol, launched in order to prevent the election of Joe Biden, by invoking historical precedent. For example, Marjorie Taylor Greene, a Republican congresswoman from Georgia, declared, 'if you think what our Declaration of Independence says, it says to overthrow tyrants'.[20] The culture war around empire, colonialism and race was far from over.

2
HOW DID WE GET HERE?

Appealing to the mythical past

Myths, as we have seen, are narratives with a political purpose. The earliest myths were founding myths, stories about how dynasties, states and empires had come into being. Rulers claimed that they were descended from gods or from ancient heroes who had consorted with gods. After the Roman Empire, the rulers of other empires claimed that they were reincarnations of Rome, with the military and civic glory that went with it. Founders of nations which defined themselves against imperial powers argued that the nation embodied a people, above all a people chosen by God. Historians have generally presented themselves as myth-busters, telling the truth about what actually happened in the past. But it has not always been as simple as that. Historians too have been guilty of myth-making, not least because, so often, myth is more seductive than truth.

In ancient Egypt between 170 and 180 pharaohs claimed to be descended from a large pantheon of gods, a claim that lasted for about 3,000 years. The pharaohs presided over the cults maintained by priests to sanctify their rule and alone could communicate with the gods. Among those gods were Osiris, the king of the dead, and his sister and wife Isis, who had healing powers. When Osiris was killed by his brother Seth, their son Horus grew up to challenge Seth for the rulership of Egypt. After long contention and appeals to other gods, Horus eventually triumphed over his uncle and became pharaoh of all Egypt.

The rulers of ancient Greece claimed descent from the gods and heroes who fought in the Trojan war, it too caused by a quarrel among gods. Homer's *Iliad*, written in the eighth or seventh century BCE, referred back to a city in Asia Minor, Troy, which acquired a particular magical significance. Herodotus, writing in the fifth century BCE, accepted the account of Egyptian priests about the truth of the abduction of Helen of Troy and suggested that the Trojan war had taken place eight hundred years before his time. Herodotus became known as 'the father of history' but the main point of the story was not its truth but the powerful myth that Greek rulers were descended from the Greek heroes of Troy.

The ancient Romans for their part claimed descent from the Trojan survivors of that war. The poet Virgil related in *The Aeneid* that Rome had been founded by Aeneas, the son of the goddess Aphrodite (Venus for the Romans) and the hero Anchises, whom Aeneas was said to have carried on his back from the burning city of Troy before he settled in Italy. Written at the beginning of the reign of the Emperor Augustus (27 BCE to 14 CE), the poem provided mythical legitimacy for the emperor and may even have been commissioned by him.

The Roman Empire, once established in Europe, the Near East and North Africa, lasted for over a thousand years and acquired a mythic power of its own. With its armies, roads, governance and culture, it came to represent civilization itself, conquering and subduing surrounding 'barbarians'. Any regime that could make out that it was a new incarnation of Rome also boasted that it would last for a thousand years.

After the fall of the Roman Empire in the West in 476 CE, the Byzantine Empire which survived in the East adopted Orthodox Christianity as its official religion and its rulers thus claimed to be sanctified by both Rome and God through the Patriarch at Constantinople. Meanwhile the 'barbarian' rulers in the West made their own claims on the Roman inheritance. Charlemagne, King of the Franks, had himself crowned by the Pope in St Peter's, Rome, on Christmas Day in 800 CE and inaugurated the Holy Roman Empire which, acting as a focus for the disparate German states, lasted for a thousand years until 1806.

The thousand years of the Byzantine Empire ended in 1453, when Constantinople was overrun by the Ottoman Turks. A claim to be a Third Rome was made by Moscow, where the grand prince Ivan III had fought back the Turkic Golden Horde, married the niece of the last Byzantine emperor in 1469 and proclaimed himself tsar. Moscow also portrayed itself as the bastion of the Orthodox Christian Church with the establishment of the Moscow Patriarchate in 1589.

In the wake of the turmoil of the French Revolution, the young general Napoleon Bonaparte proclaimed himself Emperor of the French. He was to be a new Roman emperor, having himself crowned with a replica of Charlemagne's crown, but this time it was the Pope who travelled to Paris for the ceremony. The Arc de Triomphe he had built in Paris mimicked the triumphal arches of the emperors Septimus Severus and Constantine in Rome, while the 42-metre column on which he was portrayed as a Roman emperor surpassed the 30-metre column of the Emperor Trajan.

Far from lasting a thousand years, however, Napoleon's empire lasted barely ten. It destroyed the Holy Roman Empire and provoked a backlash of German nationalism which was expressed by thousands of young Germans who volunteered to fight against the tyrant Napoleon. Far from spreading civilization, they felt, the French Empire brought only oppression and exploitation and snuffed out the right of each nation to enjoy freedom.

In the late eighteenth century, German pastor and philosopher Johann Gottfried Herder argued that each nation was defined above all by its language, the songs that its people sang and the stories they told. Those songs and stories expressed a nation's history, beliefs and sentiments, indeed its soul. In order to

Figure 2.1: *Homecoming of the Militiaman from the War of Liberation,* oil painting by Johann Peter Krafft, 1817

The patriotism of this older volunteer expressed the crystallization of German nationalism against French occupation.

define themselves as nations, peoples must elevate their spoken languages into written languages, honour their national literatures and record their histories of triumph and suffering.

The myth of the nation was powerful in a Europe which was controlled after 1815 by a concert of multinational empires – British, Prussian, Austrian, Russian and Ottoman. Within them new nations mobilized to break up the empires and found new nation states. Each of these nations needed its own story. 'History', as historian Margaret MacMillan has said, 'provides much of the fuel for nationalism.'[1] They were also keen to have God on their side and portray themselves as his chosen people. Adam Mickiewicz, in exile in Paris after the Polish revolt of 1831 was crushed by the Russians, argued that the Poles were the Christ of nations, suffering now but destined to be redeemed and to fight for other nations too. Giuseppe Mazzini, also in exile after various uprisings against Austrian and papal rule in the Italian states around 1830, developed an Italian nationalism that was inspired by 'God and the people'. František Palacký, oppressed by Austrian rule in Bohemia and Moravia, promoted the Czech language, literature and a history defined by the much earlier revolt of Jan Hus, burned at the stake for heresy in 1415. Taras Shevchenko, who spoke for the Ukrainian serfs of Polish and Russian landlords, wrote poetry derived from Ukrainian folk songs and celebrated the peasant revolt of 1768. Meanwhile the Serbs, defeated by the Ottoman Turks at the battle of Kosovo on 15 June 1389, chose the same date to launch an uprising against the Ottomans in 1876. Founding myths also had founding dates.

As empires replaced nations and nations succeeded empires so national and imperial myths changed place. When Prussia defeated the Second French Empire of Napoleon III in 1870 it declared itself to be a Second German Empire, and a victory column modelled on those of Trajan and Napoleon was unveiled in Berlin. France, meanwhile, no longer an empire but a republic, fell back on a myth that the nation embodied a common experience of heroism, suffering and solidarity that would eventually bring rebirth. In a lecture of 1882, the French intellectual Ernest Renan asked 'What is a Nation?' and gave the following answer:

> A heroic past, of great men, of glory (I mean the genuine kind), that is the social principle on which the national idea rests. To have common glories in the past, a common will in the present; to have accomplished great things together, to wish to do so again, that is the essential condition for being a nation ... common suffering is greater than happiness. In fact national sorrows are more significant than triumphs because they impose obligations and demand a common effort.[2]

Defeated in Europe, the French sought to recover national pride by building an overseas empire. They competed with Britain, Germany, Russia, Italy and the United States, which were trading empires, colonies of white settlement and territorial expansion in America, Australasia, Asia and Africa. Although this expansion involved the exploitation, expropriation and even extermination of Indigenous peoples, the myth built around colonial empire was that the Western nations were civilized and the Indigenous peoples were 'savage' or 'barbaric', so that colonies were justified in terms of their civilizing mission.

The expansion of the American frontier west and south after 1830, driving out Native Americans, was presented as a special version of the civilizing mission, Manifest Destiny. According to Irish-American journalist John L. O'Sullivan, Americans asserted the right 'to overspread and to possess the whole of the continent which Providence has given us for the development of the great experiment of liberty and federative self-government entrusted to us'.[3] A visual representation of this myth was provided in 1872 by the Berlin-born American lithographer John Gast, whose 'American Progress' depicted Columbia as a Greek goddess moving from east to west across the continent, bearing a book and telegraph wire and leading settlers in a wagon, stagecoach and railway train as Native Americans and buffalo flee before them.

The following decade, French statesman Jules Ferry defended his country's colonial expansion in pseudo-scientific terms: 'We must proclaim openly that the superior races have a right vis-à-vis the inferior races because they have a duty towards them. They have a duty to civilise them.' In 1902 Edward Elgar likewise wrote an ode for the coronation of Edward VII, the finale of which used a melody from his Pomp and Circumstance March No. 1, while the lyrics, 'Land of Hope and Glory' written by Arthur Benson, urged, 'God, who made thee mighty, make thee mightier yet'. Another side of this assumed superiority was dramatized by American artist Udo Keppler, who in the same year published a cartoon in *Puck* magazine which depicted Britannia leading red-coated troops and bearing a flag marked 'civilization' confronting a band of Africans clad only in loincloths and waving spears, under a banner marked 'barbarism'.

The racism underlying the myth of the civilizing mission was exposed by W.E.B. Du Bois, the first African American to gain a PhD and one of the founders

Figure 2.2: *From the Cape to Cairo* by Udo Keppler, cartoon from *Puck* magazine, 1902

This tribute to Britain's ambitions to build an empire across Africa is legitimated in scarcely veiled racist terms as the triumph of 'Civilization' over 'Barbarism'.

of the National Association for the Advancement of Colored People in 1909. 'What on earth is whiteness that one should so desire it?' he asked in his 1910 essay 'The Souls of White Folk'. He answered the question himself, pointing to 'this new religion of whiteness' that proclaimed its own supremacy over people of colour portrayed, in the words of Rudyard Kipling, as 'half-devil and half-child', and assumed the duty 'to divide up the darker world and to administer it for Europe's good'. According to this myth, said Du Bois, 'Whiteness is the ownership of the earth for ever and ever. Amen.'[4]

During the First World War the opposition between civilization and barbarism was used as a way of describing the European enemy. British and French propaganda denounced Germans as barbarians, accusing them of raping Belgium women, skewering their babies on bayonets and then bombarding the French cathedral of Reims, which symbolized European civilization. This propaganda was stepped up to persuade the United States to join the war. The Germans, by contrast, portrayed their own combatants as armoured crusaders and mocked British, French and Russian soldiers as weak, crippled, drunk or otherwise unmanly. When the war was lost and the German empire collapsed, replaced by the Weimar Republic, right-wing German propaganda created the myth that German armies had remained supreme on the battlefield but had been stabbed in the back by Bolshevik and Jewish conspirators, often presented as in alliance.

Adolf Hitler, a veteran of the First World War, vowed to eliminate Bolsheviks and Jews so that they could not frustrate Germany's recovery of its lost power. Germany's Third Reich was envisaged as a restoration of the Roman Empire that would also last a thousand years. German soldiers parading at a Nazi party rally carried banners in the style of Roman legions with the Roman eagle, Nazi swastika and the motto 'Germany Awakes'. Hitler's favourite architect, Albert Speer, was commissioned in 1937 to rebuild Berlin as 'Germania', the capital of Europe, if not the world. At one end of a three-mile avenue a triumphal arch would be twice the height of the Arc de Triomphe in Paris, while at the other a copper-domed Volkshalle (people's hall) with capacity for 180,000 people would be sixteen times the size of St Peter's, Rome. Because of the war, however, this fantasy remained just that.

Germany's Axis ally, Japan, had been humiliated at the Paris Peace Conference in 1919 when its bid to have a clause inserted on the racial equality of nations was rejected. The West's sense of racial superiority clashed with its own sense of its historic expansionist mission. In 1940 a young British lecturer attended the celebrations in Tokyo of the 2,600th anniversary of the foundation of Japan's imperial dynasty, said to have been descended from the sun goddess, Amaratsu.[5] This mission was pursued in the 1930s by a military, fascist and imperialist regime which led to the occupation of Manchuria (north-east China), where secret experiments in biological warfare were carried out on Chinese and Soviet prisoners, and to the invasion of China, which resulted in the massacre of tens of thousands of Chinese in Nanjing in 1937–8.

The Second World War saw national and imperial myth-making on all sides. The British developed a myth that they stood alone against Hitler and then liberated German-occupied Europe, but said much less about how the war was fought to save the British Empire. The French, defeated and occupied by the Germans, elaborated a myth that most French people resisted Hitler and said much less about the Vichy regime and its collaboration with the Nazis. The Soviet Union, meanwhile, evolved a myth of the Great Patriotic War, which drew on myths from Russia's pre-revolutionary past, epitomized by Sergei Eisenstein's films *Alexander Nevsky* and *Ivan the Terrible*. No mention was made of the Soviet Union's deportation east during the war of minority ethnic groups who were seen as a security risk, from Germans, Finns, Bulgarians and Armenians to Chechens, Crimean Tatars, Turks and Iranians.

By the 1980s, however, the most powerful narrative to emerge from the Second World War was that of the Holocaust. Unlike myths, the reality of the destruction of the European Jews has never been questioned except by a very small minority of Holocaust deniers. It has also been called the Shoah (the Hebrew word for 'catastrophe') and is recognized as genocide – the deliberate destruction in whole or in part of a national, religious, ethnic or racial group – under the United Nations Convention of 9 December 1949. Its significance was highlighted by Yad Vashem, Israel's official remembrance centre set up in Jerusalem in 1953 to commemorate the Jewish victims of Nazism, a vast amount of historical scholarship, and the United States Holocaust Memorial Museum that opened in 1993. The only aspect to be contested was how far the Holocaust was unique as an act of genocide. A conference at Yad Vashem in 1982 was racked by controversy because of the number of papers on the Armenian genocide at the hands of the Turks in 1915. In 1994 the descent of Rwanda into civil war and the massacre of a million of the Tutsi minority by the Hutu majority was commonly accepted as the worst genocide since the Holocaust.

At the turn of the twenty-first century the concept of genocide was adopted by formerly colonized countries in order to denounce the violence used against them by their former colonial masters and to demand compensation. In 2001, for example, the rulers of

Namibia, which had gained independence from South Africa in 1990, filed a demand for compensation from the German government for its massacre of the Herero and Nama peoples in 1904–05 when it controlled South-West Africa. This was now described as colonial genocide, or Germany's first holocaust. The following year, 2005, the Algerian president Abdelaziz Bouteflika demanded compensation from the French government for the massacres committed against Algerian protesters at Sétif and Guelma on 8 May 1945, the same day victory over Germany was being celebrated in Europe. In 2011 relatives of the Mau Mau resisters to British rule in Kenya in the 1950s, who had been herded into concentration camps and seen their leaders hanged, demanded compensation from the British government. Similarly, in the lead-up to the centenary of the Amritsar massacre of peaceful Punjabi protesters by the British army in 1919 the Indian government demanded an apology from the British government which has still not come.

Historians and myth

Historians have generally drawn a distinction between myth and history. Myth serves a political purpose and may distort or ignore evidence; history is faithful to the evidence and is objective, if not scientific. Historians present themselves as 'myth-busters', distinguishing myth from 'reality', writing 'new' accounts based on new sources or revising accounts of the past that are tendentious and unreliable.

Things are nevertheless more complicated than that. To begin with, historians claim that their accounts are objective, even scientific accounts, but at the same time they often see themselves as storytellers who prioritize plot and characters. Some historians, moreover, have been close to political power as 'court' or 'official' historians and have written histories supportive of those in power. Others, out of power and challenging it, have seen it as their responsibility to critique the half-truths spun by power.

In ancient Greece, Herodotus gathered his information from a variety of sources, mainly the oral testimony from Greeks and non-Greeks, and weighed up how credible they were. 'Of all the many stories that were told of Cyrus' death', he wrote, 'this one seems to me the most credible' (*Histories*, I, 214). Four hundred years later, however, the Roman statesman and historian Cicero was not so complimentary about his predecessor's method: 'There are countless fables in Herodotus, the father of history', he warned (*On the Laws*, I, 5).

Thucydides, an Athenian historian, wrote a history of the Peloponnesian war virtually as it happened. He criticized Homer's account of the Trojan war because, he said, 'as a poet he may have exaggerated for effect' (*War of the Peloponnesians and the Athenians*, 1.10). He distinguished his own account from 'the songs of the poets who exaggerate things for artistic purposes [and] the writings of the chroniclers which are composed more to make good listening than to represent the truth', citing his own 'utmost concern for accuracy' (1.22). But he was happy to give verbatim accounts of speeches which he could not remember or which had not been recorded at the time. One of his most famous was the speech he attributed to Pericles in 431 BCE in honour of the men who had died for their city in the Peloponnesian war, which suggested that for him history was very much a school of patriotism.

Tacitus, the first-century Roman official and historian, relied for his account of Germany on previous works by Caesar and the Elder Pliny, and conversations with traders and soldiers. He credited the Germans with celebrating descent from an 'earth-born god', Tuisto, but also subscribed to myths that Germany was visited by the mythical Hercules and Ulysses. The accounts of the military tactics, government, religion and customs of various German tribes read like the work of a serious researcher, but he had little evidence for tribes living in present-day Poland. 'Everything after this point is in the realm of fable', he admitted. 'The Hellusii and Oxiones are said to have human faces and features, the bodies and limbs of animals. As this has not been confirmed, I shall leave the matter open.'6

In the twelfth century Geoffrey of Monmouth, writing a *History of the Kings of Britain under the Normans*, was above all creating a founding myth. He argued that Brutus, the great-grandson of Aeneas, had been told by the goddess Diana to find an island beyond Gaul that was inhabited only by giants and there to found a new kingdom that would become a second Troy. He wove into his history the prophecies of Merlin and the deeds of King Arthur, who was said to have conquered Denmark and Norway, Gaul and Aquitaine, before he was betrayed. Among the kings of Britain, he listed the mythical King Lear.

A great step forward in the writing of scientific history took place after the French Revolution. The rule of absolute monarchs, feudal lords and priests was gone, and a new world of liberty, democracy and nationhood beckoned. The gulf between past and present opened up a space for history to examine what had gone before with a cool, objective gaze. History-writing was conceived as different from the increasingly popular genre of the historical novel. This was fictional but, in the case of the Scottish novelist Sir Walter Scott, also played on real historic tensions such as between the Scots and the English in *Waverley* (1814), or between the 'two hostile races' of Normans and Anglo-Saxons in *Ivanhoe* (1820).[7]

In 1824 German historian Ranke laid down the law about what objective or scientific history was. His *History of the Latin and Teutonic Nations since 1494* famously declared that 'History has had ascribed to it the duty of judging the past and instructing the present for the benefit of future ages. The present endeavour does not presume to take on such lofty responsibilities: it seeks only to show what actually happened.'[8] He argued that the main role of history was not to divide rulers into good and bad, nor to educate future generations, but in the first instance simply to record facts. This meant that the historian must use the archival records of church and state to document their work and not indulge in flights of fancy for which

2.1: The historical novel

Hungarian philosopher György Lukács argued in 1937 that the historical novel of Walter Scott was invented at the same time as the scientific history of Leopold von Ranke and that both were a response to the clear rupture between past and present that resulted from the French Revolution and Napoleonic wars. Characters and plot could now be woven into dramatic historical narratives that captured the transitions between an old world, such as the Middle Ages or Renaissance, and a new one. The historical novel could compensate for gaps in the historical record by inventing new scenarios, combining real historical figures with invented ones. The novel could invent reality because it aspired to artistic truth, not historical accuracy. It could also play freely with different forms of narrative. Works of history may also be imaginative and experiment with narrative, but they are anchored in a scholarly and critical approach to the historical evidence.

there was no evidence. He criticized Walter Scott for relying on the memoirs of Philippe de Comines for his extravagant portrayal of the French king Louis XI as a cruel and debauched tyrant in his novel *Quentin Durward* (1823). From now on, the emphasis was on using reliable sources and not making claims without solid archival evidence.

Promoted to a professorship at the University of Berlin, Ranke used the Prussian, Austrian and

Italian archives to write *The Popes of Rome in the Sixteenth and Seventeenth Centuries* (1834–36). His vaunted historical accuracy, however, did not exempt him from telling a powerful story of the rise of the German nation from the tribes described by Tacitus. Adopting a teleological approach he fast-forwarded to the Reformation, tracing the rise of Protestant Europe at the expense of the Popes and the Catholic Counter-Reformation, the rise of nation states like Prussia at the expense of the Holy Roman Empire, and the construction of a balance of power to prevent Louis XIV establishing a universal monarchy. His histories opened the way to the so-called 'Prussian school' of historians, who told the story of the rise of the Prussian state in support of Otto von Bismarck's ambition of German unification. Shortly after that was achieved, one of its number, Heinrich von Treitschke, was rewarded by Bismarck with a chair in history at the University of Berlin in 1873. He went on publish a four-volume *German History* between 1879 and 1889 which preached up the German nation under Protestant, Prussian leadership and criticized its rivals: Austria, Catholics, socialists and, increasingly, Jews.

The 'Rankean revolution' of objective, scientific history spread to other universities in Europe and America, and in theory, at least, widened the gap between history and myth. The two caveats nevertheless persisted. Not all history was written by academics and even their histories sometimes contained myth rather than history, or tendentious assertions that were unsupported by the evidence. This was often because they were close to those in power and were using history to assert legitimacy of those in power.

In England this revolution was confirmed with the appointment to the regius chairs of modern history in Oxford and Cambridge after 1860 of scholars disposed to serious critical scholarship.[9] William Stubbs, a clergyman and Lambeth Palace librarian, became regius professor in Oxford in 1866 and founded the modern history undergraduate degree in 1872. Meanwhile in Cambridge J.R. Seeley, appointed regius professor in Cambridge in 1869, introduced the history Tripos (undergraduate degree) in 1873. The history they wrote, however, was essentially a 'Whig' history which in a rather nationalistic way traced English liberty back to the Anglo-Saxons and forward to parliamentary government and the expansion of empire. Stubbs contributed through his *Select Charters of English Constitutional History* (1870) and three-volume *Constitutional History of England* (1874–78). His successor at Oxford, Edward Augustus Freeman, argued in his six-volume *History of the Norman Conquest* (1867–79) that the freedoms of the Anglo-Saxons were not obliterated by the Normans but reappeared in the medieval parliaments. He drew on a cult of the Anglo-Saxon race as free and strong in their essence, which had been launched by solicitor–historian Sharon Turner in his *History of the Anglo-Saxons* (1799–1804) and on whom Walter Scott also relied. Turner highlighted the importance of the Anglo-Saxon Witan, or assembly of wise men, which became the English parliament, 'an example and instrument of national prosperity and power, exceeded by no preceding state and equalled by very few'.[10] In Cambridge, Seeley carried the English story outward, publishing *The Expansion of England* (1885), which held that, with the exception of India, the empire was simply 'Greater Britain', 'an extension of the English nationality' built on a community of Anglo-Saxon blood, Protestant religion and economic interest.

2.2: Whig history

The Whig faction (and later political party) were liberal aristocrats who were the dominant political force in Great Britain between the 1680s and 1860s. Whig history, by extension, was the dominant school of historical writing in this period. It taught that Britain was exceptional in that it avoided both royal absolutism and revolution so prevalent on the Continent, and upheld Protestantism against Roman Catholicism associated with that absolutism. It postulated that British history was continuous, gradual and embodied progress. At its core was tracing the development of parliamentary rule and constitutional monarchy from the Anglo-Saxon Witan and Magna Carta to the Glorious Revolution of 1688 and the Great Reform Act of 1832. Abroad, it claimed that the British Empire spread free trade, Christianity and civilization. It was criticized as ideological and oversimplifying by Herbert Butterfield in *The Whig Interpretation of History* (1931).

In the United States historians were influenced both by the German scientific model and by English Anglo-Saxonism. Herbert Baxter Adams studied at Heidelberg and taught from 1878 at Johns Hopkins University, which was committed to the Rankean approach. There he wrote *The Germanic Origin of New England Towns* (1802). One of his students at Johns Hopkins, Frederick Jackson Turner, published a paper in 1893 on 'The Significance of the Frontier in American History', which set up an opposition between pioneers bearing civilization and the 'savagery' of the wild. American history, both within and outside the universities, developed the themes of expansion, civilization and, indeed, the providential mission of Manifest Destiny. Hubert Howe Bancroft, himself a pioneer who went with the gold rush to California in 1848, wrote a massive history of the Pacific Coast from the arrival of the Spanish in 1542 to 1890.[11] Julian Hawthorne, son of novelist Nathaniel Hawthorne, said at the outset of his *History of the United States from 1492 to 1910* that 'the American nation is the embodiment and vehicle of a Divine purpose to emancipate and enlighten the human race'.[12]

In France the Rankean revolution arrived in 1898 when Sorbonne professors Charles-Victor Langlois and Charles Seignobos announced in their *Introduction to the Study of History* that 'The historian works with documents. Documents are the traces which have been left by the thoughts and actions of men of former times.'[13] Since the defeat of 1870 at the hands of the Prussians, however, French historians had also been taking the advice of Renan to rebuild national spirit by underlining both the unity and continuity of French history. Another Sorbonne professor, Ernest Lavisse, dealt with the loss of Alsace-Lorraine to Germany in 1871 by presenting it as a brief episode in a millennial struggle between France and Germany that went back to the division of Charlemagne's empire in 843. Albert Sorel, who became professor of diplomatic history at the new École Libre des Sciences Politiques (now better known as 'Sciences Po'), wrote a multi-volume work on *Europe and the French Revolution* (1885–1904), which showed that French ambitions in the revolutionary and Napoleonic periods were part of the same thousand-year Franco-German rivalry. Gabriel Hanotaux, who was both French foreign minister in the 1890s and a historian, later wrote a patriotic *History of the French Nation* (1913) and *History of French Colonies and of French Expansion in the World* (1929–34).

The Rankean gauntlet was again picked up in England in 1903 when J.B. Bury, Anglo-Irish historian of the Roman and Byzantine empires, argued in his inaugural lecture as regius professor in Cambridge that 'history is a science, no less and no more'. This view was strongly opposed, however, by rival Cambridge historian George Macaulay Trevelyan, who resigned his college fellowship on the grounds that he regarded history as a branch of literature. His *English Social History*, published in 1942, which surveyed the ages of Chaucer, Caxton, Shakespeare, Defoe, Dr Johnson, William Cobbett and Queen Victoria, betrayed a nostalgia for Merrie England and played powerfully into a chauvinistic wartime spirit. This chauvinism was reinforced by popular historian Arthur Bryant, whose *English Saga, 1840–1940* described England as 'an island fortress ... fighting a war of redemption, not only for Europe but for her own soul' and by the young A.L. Rowse, who published *The Spirit of English History*.[14]

2.3: Merrie England

Merrie England is an imaginary golden age of an England before the Reformation, which clamped down on fun, and the industrial revolution, which took the working population away from the land. It was an England that was constantly celebrating saints' days with drinking, dancing and games. It idealized harmonious social relations between lords, yeomen and peasants and foregrounded mythical or real rebels such as Robin Hood, Wat Tyler and Shakespeare's Falstaff. After the industrial revolution it became a nostalgic reference point, found, for example, in William Blake's 'green and pleasant land', William Morris's Arts and Crafts movement and Robert Blatchford's attempt to sell socialism to workers as a return to the community life in his *Merrie England* (1893). Morris dances, country pubs, cricket, detective novels and television series such as Agatha Christie's *Miss Marple*, James Herriot's stories of a Yorkshire vet, Richard Curtis's *Blackadder*, and *The Vicar of Dibley* arguably hark back implicitly to Merrie England.

The Second World War, which mobilized and destroyed nations and empires, provided new challenges for history-writing. In countries on the Allied side, it was relatively easy to assert the continuity of national history and to see the war as a climax and justification. For defeated countries such as Germany and Japan, there was a sense that the last century or two of their history had ended in national catastrophe.

In Britain, patriotic historians with wide readerships continued their work. Arthur Bryant published *The Age of Elegance*, about the Regency, in 1950 and *The Story of England: Makers of the Realm* in 1953. A.L. Rowse brought out a trilogy on *The Elizabethan Age*: *The England of Elizabeth* (1950), *The Expansion of Elizabethan England* (1955) and *The Elizabethan Renaissance* (1971–72). Winston Churchill, who was alleged to have said that 'history will be kind to me because I will write it', published his account of *The Second World War* in six volumes (1948–54), the tone being given by the title of volume two, *Their Finest Hour*. He went on to publish a four-volume *History of the English-Speaking Peoples* (1956–58), including the so-called 'White Dominions' of Canada, South Africa, Australia and New Zealand, up to 1900.

There were, nevertheless, warnings about this gushing celebration of Britain's past playing on a nostalgia for imaginary golden ages of bygone days. Herbert Butterfield, the Master of Peterhouse Cambridge, suggested in 1955 that 'It is possible for historians to mislead a nation in respect of what it might regard as its historic mission. It is possible for them to give a wrong notion of what they can do with their destiny'.[15] Similarly, Boyd C. Schafer, editor of the *American Historical Review*, cautioned against 'illusions' of nationalism that claimed that certain nations were chosen by God and had a providential vocation. 'Nationalism', he said, 'may be in part founded on myth but myths like other errors have a way of perpetuating themselves and of becoming not true but real'.[16]

A spate of writings critiquing nationalism were published in the 1980s. Political scientist Benedict Anderson, an expert on multi-ethnic Indonesia, argued that nations were not given in any way, but 'imagined communities'. Anthropologist Ernest Gellner also stated that nations were not natural or God-given but myths. He defined nationalism as a political struggle to ensure that each state should be supported by a nation and each nation be defended by a state. At the same time, historian of Europe Eric Hobsbawm and historian of Zimbabwe Terence Ranger edited *The Invention of Tradition* (1983), which argued that traditions that claimed to be old, such as wearing kilts, singing folk songs and crowning monarchs, were more likely to be recent inventions with the purpose of binding groups together and legitimating their actions.[17]

One such invention to be exposed was Britain's myth of 1940. Clive Ponting, a civil servant at the Ministry of Defence who had been sent for trial under the Official Secrets Act for leaking documents about the sinking of the Argentinian battleship *General Belgrano* during the Falklands War, published *1940: Myth and Reality* in 1990. He brought together and popularized a good deal of research that was already questioning myth. He asserted that Churchill had sounded out Mussolini in May 1940 about a compromise peace with Germany, Dunkirk had been a disaster, the Battle of Britain had been won by geography more than heroism, and far from being united and 'keeping calm and carrying on' (a slogan not used at the time) the British people had been divided and demoralized. This line of attack was continued by David Reynolds' *In Command of History* (2004), which pointed out that by stating in *Their Finest Hour* that a negotiated settlement was never discussed in cabinet in May 1940 Churchill was guilty of a 'significant cover-up'.[18]

In France the myth of national resistance held fast for 20 years after the Second World War. Histories of resistance were churned out by former *résistants* who were keen to claim their place in history. The experience of the collaborationist Vichy regime was forgotten or whitewashed. Historian Robert Aron argued in 1954 that the Vichy of 1940–42 had been benign and protected the French, whereas only that of 1942–44 had openly collaborated with the Germans and deported Jews. The myth-busting came in 1972 from American historian Robert Paxton, who argued in *Vichy France* that the regime had sought rather than suffered collaboration with the Germans in order to benefit from Hitler's Europe. His verdict was widely criticized by French historians until in 1987 Henry Rousso's *Vichy Syndrome* reopened the debate on the nature and significance of the period. Meanwhile other historians began to examine the resistance more closely. Some argued that only a fraction of French people engaged in active resistance, others that many in the 'French' resistance were Spanish republicans, Italian anti-fascists, Polish Jews or British agents.

2.4: Revisionism

History is both what happened in the past and what historians write about what happened. Some people deny that some events, such as the Holocaust, or Joe Biden's election victory in 2020, actually took place. Historians accept these as fact, but what and how they write about them changes over time. They are constantly revising what has been written, a process known as revisionism.

Revisionism happens for a number of reasons. Historians may find new sources or reassess existing ones. The historical context changes, so that histories written before the Cold War or 9/11 will differ from those written after. New disciplines and sub-disciplines are introduced, such as women's history, gender history, global history and Black history. New questions are asked of history, such as 'What is the legacy of colonialism?'. On this and other questions historians will disagree and may be in rivalry with each other. They will wish to dismiss 'received opinion' and 'traditional views' and to persuade colleagues and the public to accept their 'new' or 'original' interpretation. Revising history is what they do for a living.

If the past was difficult to deal with in France, in the Federal Republic of Germany it was almost impossible. How might historians deal with German history since the time of Ranke that had ended with such a catastrophe? Gerhard Ritter, a veteran of the First World War and aged 30 when the empire collapsed in 1918, drew a sharp distinction between Bismarck and imperial Germany which, he argued, had limited military aims, and Nazi Germany, which was totalitarian and controlled by a criminal clique and a madman. He clashed in 1961 with a younger historian, Fritz Fischer, who claimed that Germany's grasp for world domination did not begin in 1933 but was already evident in imperial Germany in 1914. Fischer also claimed that the roots of Nazi Germany went back to Bismarck's time and that Germany had taken a *Sonderweg* (different path) from that of liberal, capitalist European powers. Because Germany had missed out on a liberal revolution, he argued, the contradiction between its advanced industrial development and backward feudal–monarchical political system had had to be resolved by an imperialistic foreign policy and the persecution of the Jewish and socialist 'enemy within'.

Controversy about the history of Nazi Germany erupted again in 1985 when President Reagan met Chancellor Helmut Kohl in Germany and in Bitburg cemetery honoured the German war dead, who included soldiers of the Waffen-SS. German historians who were keen to escape from hand-wringing guilt about Nazi history saw this as an opportunity to 'normalize' their response to their country's past and feel pride in it again. There followed the so-called *Historikerstreit* or Historians' Dispute, in which apologists of Nazi German history lined up against their critics. On one side, nationalist and anti-communist historian Ernst Nolte argued that Nazi Germany must be explained as a response to the Bolshevik Revolution and Stalin's crimes: Hitler's concentration camps were no worse than the Gulags, and racial genocide was no worse than class genocide. On the other, Jürgen Habermas argued that Nolte and others were in effect writing a defence of Nazi history and that Germany's membership of the European Community depended on a critical assessment of its past, however painful.

In Japan there was, arguably, an even greater reluctance to accept responsibility for atrocities perpetrated in the Second World War. A critical approach was taken by Saburō Ienaga, a professor at Tokyo's University of Education, who had his *New Japanese History* school textbook refused for publication as unpatriotic by the Ministry of Education in 1963. He responded by giving lectures in 1965 on Japan's war from the invasion of Manchuria in 1931 to 1945 and took the government to court three times for its 'screening' or censorship of school textbooks. *Japan's Last War*, published in English in 1979, provided evidence of the Japanese Rape of Nanking in 1937, the drafting of Korean slave labour for the Japanese economy and as 'comfort girls' for Japanese soldiers, and the illegal bacteriological warfare experiments conducted on prisoners by Unit 731 in Harbin, Manchuria.

Although the Allied powers made capital out of their resistance to Nazism, they did not go scot-free. In time, criticism of their role as imperial and colonial powers caught up with them. This did not happen straight away. Gallagher and Robinson's *Africa and the Victorians* (1967) explained *how* rather than *why* the British Empire had expanded in Egypt and South Africa, that is, in order to safeguard the route to India. Indigenous revolts were given as a reason for extending power and their suppression was scarcely mentioned. Decolonization in the 1960s was generally explained as a peaceful transfer of power to colonial elites who had long been prepared for self-government, not as a liberation through violence from the colonial order.

These views were transformed by the emergence of a postcolonial history which analysed empire from the viewpoint not of the colonizer but of the colonized. Three interventions by writers – not necessarily historians – stood out. The first of these was *The Wretched of the Earth* (1961, first published in English in 1963) by Martinique-born psychiatrist and intellectual Frantz Fanon, whose experience of French colonization in Algeria taught him that colonialism was based on the dehumanization of the colonized peoples as savages, justifying the use of violence, including torture, and that only violence against the colonizers could restore the integrity of the colonized.[19] The second was *Orientalism* (1978) by Edward Said, an intellectual of Palestinian origin working in the United States, who argued that since

Napoleon landed in Egypt in 1798, the West had systematically characterized the Arab and Islamic world as weak, effeminate, factional, cruel and unable to reform itself in order to justify extending imperial power over it and seeking to modernize it.[20] Third, there was the school of 'subaltern studies', which focused on peasants, workers, tradesmen and other groups who defied the colonial elite. It was epitomized by Ranajit Guha, born in Bengal, who edited 'Writings in South Asian History and Society' from 1982 and published *Elementary Aspects of Peasant Insurgency in Colonial India* (1983). The challenge was taken up by – among others – Gayatri Chakravorty Spivak, a Calcutta-born scholar who pursued her academic career in the United States and in 1988 published the essay 'Can the Subaltern Speak?'. This demonstrated that the history of empire had been written by empire-builders from their own archives, silenced the colonized and imposed their own interpretation. She argued, for example, that while it was impossible to recuperate women's voices about *sati*, it was not simply a barbaric Indian practice that had had to be eliminated by the British 'white men saving brown women from brown men'. It was rather an 'ideological battleground' between Hindu families keen to assert rights over property that might otherwise go to the widow, and the free choice of the widow in pursuit of an ideal of womanly conduct.[21]

The postcolonial approach to empire did not go unchallenged. It stirred up controversy among historians that amounted to a culture war. For what

2.5: Historical frames or lenses

History may be studied using a number of frames, sometimes called lenses, which relate to geography and viewpoint. They may be simply methodological but may also be political. One standard frame is national and concentrates on a country's government and society. Another is colonial or imperial, exploring the expansion of a nation or nations through migration, trade, investment and rule. Borders and border disputes may be central to this. Rather different is global history, which focuses on the movement and interplay of people, goods and ideas. It follows ways in which they cross and sometimes subvert borders. Related to global history is transnational history, which examines connections between (for example) activists or fighters between countries. They may explore how encounters give rise to both understandings and misunderstandings. Postcolonial history adopts the perspective of the subjects of colonization, not only in the colonies but also in metropoles to which they migrated. Eco-history, finally, starts and finishes with the environment and the impact of humans on it.

was at stake was not only historical interpretation – which historians were more faithful to the evidence. It was about who got to tell the history of empire, where they stood in relation to the dominant civilizing narrative of those who held power: a battle, in a word, between white history and Black history.

The culture war took off after Afghan guerrilla fighters successfully ended the Soviet occupation of their country in 1989, the first Gulf War of 1991, the 9/11 attacks on New York and Washington, and British and American intervention in Afghanistan and Iraq. Anti-Islamism was now used to give legitimacy to a New Imperialism by the US, Britain and France in the Middle East. The British Orientalist and Princeton academic Bernard Lewis published 'The Roots of Muslim Rage' in *The Atlantic* in September 1990; the cover picture of the edition showed a turbaned figure, staring angrily out at the reader.[22] Harvard professor Samuel Huntington claimed in a 1993 essay and more fully in a 1996 book that after the end of Cold War, conflicts would be clashes of civilizations, fired by opposing religious and cultural identities, in which the free and 'civilized' world would have to defend itself.[23] In *Empire* (2003) Niall Ferguson suggested that the British Empire had been an exercise in 'Anglobalization', bringing trade, white settlement, Protestantism and good governance to a quarter of the world. He concluded that 'just like the British empire before it, the American Empire unfailingly acts in the name of liberty'.[24] Two years later he published *Colossus*, which remade the case for a 'self-conscious American imperialism'. Americans, he conceded, had always refused to admit that they ran an empire, but argued that 'they do aspire to have others rule themselves in the American way' of democracy and capitalism.[25]

The descent of the Iraq war into a war of colonial occupation and resistance provided a context in which the violence of empire could be reconsidered. David Anderson and Caroline Elkins each exposed the atrocities committed by the British in Kenya in the 1950s as they sought to cling on to empire, Anderson calling his book *Histories of the Hanged* and Elkins titling hers *Britain's Gulag*.[26] Andrew Roberts accused Elkins of a 'blood libel' against the British people and riposted in 2006 with *A History of the English Speaking Peoples since 1900*, which offered a fifth and final volume of Churchill's oeuvre.[27]

Meanwhile, in France, there was a revived fear that immigrant populations, particularly those of Muslim origin, would overrun the so-called 'Français de souche', whose birthrate was falling. In 2011 there was, however, something of a mood shift. Jean Raspail's dystopic novel *The Camp of the Saints* (1973), which foretold an armada of a thousand ships and a million migrants landing on the south coast of France, was republished with a new preface warning that 'The most exotic ethnic groups, tribes and nationalities are banging on our gates and when they have forced them their heritage is assured'. By 2050, he predicted, over 50 per cent of those living in France would be of extra-European origin unless this was stopped by 'a sort of *Reconquista*'.[28] This book was the favourite reading of Front National leader and French presidential candidate Marine Le Pen, who recommended it to Steve Bannon, chief strategist of Donald Trump.[29] Meanwhile another veteran reactionary, Renaud Camus, published *Le Grand Remplacement*, which issued the same warning that the French people were being 'replaced' by immigrants.[30]

What became known as the Great Replacement Theory, provided with additional ammunition by the migration crisis of 2015, gave succour to defenders of a white, Christian West. In 2017 Bruce Gilley, a professor of political science at Portland State University, published a paper on 'The Case for Colonialism' in *Third World Quarterly* which suggested that colonialism had been based on good governance and a civilizing mission and should be tried again. Withdrawn after two petitions from hostile academics were submitted, it was subsequently republished in *Academic Questions*.[31] The cause was taken up in the same year by Nigel Biggar of the University of Oxford, who launched an 'Ethics and Empire' project. This rebooted the civilizing mission, argued that the British Empire had been good as well as bad, and claimed that what was at stake in the debate was 'the moral authority of the West'.

Against this offensive were ranged a succession of postcolonial critiques: *Inglorious Empires* (2017) by former Indian minister Shashi Tharoor, who argued that the British plundered India and ruthlessly divided to rule; *Insurgent Empire* by Cambridge academic Priyamvada Gopal, who chronicled colonial resistance to the British Empire and showed how this was supported by British radicals; and *Time's Monster* by Stanford historian Priya Satia, who argued that after the Indian Mutiny of 1857 British rule replaced liberal reform by repression, an ideology of racial superiority and inferiority and a new arrogance of empire. Satia aptly quoted George Bernard Shaw, who in his 1897 play *The Man of Destiny* put into the mouth of Napoleon the opinion that the Englishman is 'never at a loss for an effective moral attitude … you will never find an Englishman in the wrong'.[32]

Caroline Elkins returned to the fray with *Legacy of Violence* in 2022, drawing on the revelation in 2011 that the British government had either destroyed or locked away colonial records that left traces of its atrocities, arguing that 'violence was inherent to liberalism' and that through emergency measures and martial law the empire was based on 'legalised lawlessness'.[33] Not to be defeated, Nigel Biggar's *Colonialism* (2023) attacked the 'anti-colonialists' and highlighted the 'liberal, humanitarian principles and endeavours of the colonial past that deserve to be admired, owned and carried into the future'.[34]

Builders of empires and nations have often resorted to historical myth, arguing that they were descended from Troy or Rome, or were the bearers of civilization in one form or another. The task of the historian is to critique, if not to bust, such myths, often to expose the power play behind such claims and ambitions. Problems arise when historians themselves become involved in myth-making, not least because they are not always in ivory towers but are themselves close to power. New generations of historians, with other evidence and other approaches, must come along to critique and bust the latest round of myth-making.

History and power: the struggle for legitimacy

To return to George Orwell: 'Who controls the past', ran the Party slogan in *Nineteen Eighty-Four*,[35] 'controls the future: who controls the present controls the past.' Historical accounts are used by all regimes to legitimate the power they have taken and hold. Models and precedents drawn from history lend authority to power, building support by demonstrating that those who hold power should hold it, by rights. They often use a teleological model, not only justifying their power in the present but projecting it forward, creating a vision of the future to which they are driving. Legitimacy builds consent over the long term.

That said, power is always contested. There is resistance, rebellion, even revolution. Revolutions create a theoretical problem, because they are replacing the regime that went before and so cannot or do not wish to appeal to tradition or precedent. They may instead appeal to a status quo ante, the situation that prevailed before the one that has been replaced. Thus revolutionaries in the modern period often argued that they were a new edition of the Roman republic, which overthrew tyrants. They also dared, however, to reject history altogether and to argue that they were founding a new order based on first principles. Defenders of monarchical power argue that authority is bestowed from above, by some heavenly or godlike power. Defenders of democratic power argue that it comes from below, conferred by the people and enshrining the rights of man. In this sense revolutions created a new legitimacy and argued that history was now starting again, with the brave new world they were founding.

This chapter explores the use of history on two levels. The first level explores the use of history by those in power and those close to them, seeking to legitimate them. The second level analyses the historians of regimes and revolutions, who may be writing a history 'as it actually was', but are likely themselves to be more or less sympathetic to the regime in place. As historian E.H. Carr said in 1961, 'when we take up a work of history, our first concern should be not with the facts which it contains but with the historian who wrote it'.[36] Historians, of course, are entangled in webs of power. They may be court historians or official historians; they may be dissident historians or radical historians. They will be arguing with each other, keen to have their interpretation accepted and that of rival historians dismissed. Not least, they are shaped by their historical context. This may be that of English, American or French Revolution, the Revolutions of 1848, the American Civil War, the Cold War or the Civil Rights movement.

Ancient empires, medieval monarchies, modern revolutions

In China, for thousands of years, the emperor was held to be a mediator between heaven and earth with a Mandate of Heaven to rule his people well. If things did not go well and there were floods, droughts, famine and civil strife, then it was clear that the emperor had lost his sacred mandate and that this should now pass to someone who successfully claimed the imperial title. The doctrine of the Mandate of Heaven was first developed by the Zhou dynasty, which overthrew the Shang dynasty in about 1050 BCE. From the Han dynasty of 202 BCE to 220 CE, the doctrine was reinforced by the Confucian ethic which prescribed the obedience of children to fathers, women to men and subjects to the emperor. Later, the Ming dynasty (1368–1644) and Qing dynasty of Manchu conquerors (1644–1911) also claimed the mandate.

In medieval and early modern Europe, the most common legitimation of monarchical power was the doctrine of the divine right of kings. This held that monarchs were divinely ordained and that generally their succession should be hereditary. The historical authority they claimed was biblical, citing the prophet Samuel's declaration to the people of Israel that God had set first Saul and then David to rule over them, and disobedience to the king was considered tantamount to disobedience to God. Unlike the Mandate of Heaven, the divine right of kings asserted that it did not come with strings attached; instead, subjects were constrained unconditionally. Given this supreme authority, divine right monarchs were inclined to claim absolute power, free of the constraints of custom or representative institutions. At the opening of the English parliament in 1397 Chancellor Edmund Stafford, Bishop of Exeter, sought to reinforce the power of Richard II by quoting Ezekiel 37:22: 'There shall be one king over all'. This, he argued, required that 'first, the king should be powerful enough to govern; secondly, his law should be properly executed; and thirdly, that his subjects should be obedient'.[37]

Those who overthrew imperial or monarchical power had to seek legitimacy from another historical model. This was initially the Roman republic, which ran from the expulsion of the Tarquin kings around 507 BCE to Augustus Caesar's proclamation of himself as emperor in 31 BCE. *The History of Rome* written by Titus Livius, known as Livy, praised the body of Roman citizens who also served as soldiers, institutions such as the senate and tribunes of the people who protected liberty, and a civil religion that cultivated civic virtue and patriotism. Normally two consuls held executive power, but provision was made in times of crisis for the appointment of a short-term dictator. There was always a danger that a dictator would exceed their powers and destroy liberty; the assassination of the dictator Julius Caesar in 44 BCE by a group of senators led by Brutus became a reference point for later republicans who were committed to the defence of liberty against the threat of tyranny.

During the Renaissance the Roman republican model was turned to by humanist thinkers in Italian city states who were looking to defend those republics against the pretensions of princely families. Machiavelli, who served the Florentine republic between the expulsion of the Medici princes in 1494 and their return in 1512, rediscovered Livy and wrote his *Discourses* as a commentary on Livy's *History*. 'Those who have displayed prudence in constituting a republic', he wrote, 'have looked upon the safeguarding of liberty

Figure 2.3: *Assassination of Julius Caesar,* **drawing by Vincenzo Camuccini, 1793–96, pen and brown ink with brush and grey wash over graphite**

The leading role of Brutus in the murder of Julius Caesar in 44 BCE was long used to legitimate the killing of tyrants in the name of liberty.

as one of the most essential things which this had to provide' (Book I, ch. 5). He underlined the importance of civic virtue or patriotism, armies formed by citizens (since mercenary armies were regarded as the tool of dictators) and a civil religion that underpinned the state (unlike the Catholic Church, which, for him, taught subservience and divided Italy).

The English Civil War

In the early seventeenth century, European monarchs keen to secure themselves against political, religious and social unrest revived the doctrine of the divine right of kings. James VI of Scotland and I of England warned Parliament in 1609 not to challenge him because, as he put it, 'The state of monarchy is the supremest thing upon earth; for kings are not only God's lieutenants upon earth, and sit upon God's throne, but even by God himself are called gods.' Defenders of the common law and parliament, by contrast, keen to check the attempts of James I and Charles I to promote absolute monarchy, found historical justification for their view in what they called 'the ancient constitution', the body of parliamentary statutes limiting royal power. James's Lord Chief Justice Sir Edward Coke argued that 'the king has no prerogative but that which the law of the land allows him' and that law was the Anglo-Saxon law, which had been confirmed by the Normans, and culminated in King John's signing of Magna Carta in 1215. 'Magna Carta', declared Coke, 'is such a fellow that he will have no sovereign'.[38]

As Britain descended into civil war in the 1640s, more radical activists such as the Levellers argued that this 'ancient constitution' was simply Norman law that defended the interests of feudal lords, while Magna Carta was 'but a beggarly thing, containing many marks of intolerable bondage'. They developed the rival historical doctrine of the Norman Yoke and said that its laws must be repealed in order to restore the liberties of freeborn Englishmen enjoyed by the Anglo-Saxons before 1066.[39]

After the execution of Charles I in 1649 and the establishment of an English Commonwealth or

Republic under a Council of State, there was a reversion to Roman republican ideas of liberty. The poet John Milton, who had studied Livy and Machiavelli, was appointed the Commonwealth's secretary for foreign tongues and wrote a *Defence of the People of England* (1651) in which he declared that 'it is clear that all the most outstanding men among the Romans not only killed tyrants in whatever way and whenever they could but that, like the Greeks formerly, they held that deed as worthy of the greatest praise'.[40]

After the fall of the Republic and the restoration of the monarchy in 1660, the victors had the first opportunity to write the history of the Civil War. Edward Hyde, who had briefly tried to reconcile king and parliament in 1640–41, became an adviser to Charles I and architect of the Restoration, when Charles II made him Earl of Clarendon. His history, published in 1702–04, attacked the legitimacy of parliament's position by calling it *The History of the Great Rebellion*. He did not mince his words about the execution of Charles I, calling it 'the most execrable murder that ever was committed since that of our blessed Saviour'.[41]

The suppression of republican views after the Restoration meant that a more sympathetic history of the Civil War took an even longer time to emerge. Catharine Macaulay, a Kent landowner's daughter and wife of a Scottish physician, who had studied the Greek and Roman republics and opposed what she saw as the royal tyranny and corrupt, aristocratic parliament of George III, wrote *The History of England from the Accession of James I to the Revolution* between

1763 and 1783. On Charles I she echoed Milton's radical view that 'kings, the servants of the state, when they degenerated into tyrants, forfeited their right to government' and called the Commonwealth 'the brightest age that ever adorned the page of history'.[42]

Monarchical tyranny and corruption in the British Empire were also opposed by American colonists who, in the lead-up to their revolution and War of Independence, initially drew legitimacy from classical Rome. They saw themselves as 'new Romans' steeped in civic virtue and patriotism, throwing off the rule of George III, who was portrayed as the evil emperor Nero. The 1776 Declaration of Independence asserted that 'the history of the present King of Great Britain is a history of repeated injuries and usurpations, all having in direct object the establishment of an absolute Tyranny over these states'. At the same time, however, the fact that the American Revolution was opening up a new chapter in human history made reference to the past less necessary. The Declaration of Independence announced that:

> We hold these truths to be self-evident, that all men are created equal, that they are endowed by their Creator with certain unalienable Rights, that among these are Life, Liberty and the pursuit of Happiness. – That to secure these rights, Governments are instituted among Men, deriving their just powers from the consent of the governed.

The great seal of the United States in 1782 used a Latin motto – *novus ordo seclorum* (the new order

Figure 2.4: The Declaration of Independence, first printed version, produced by John Dunlap, 1776

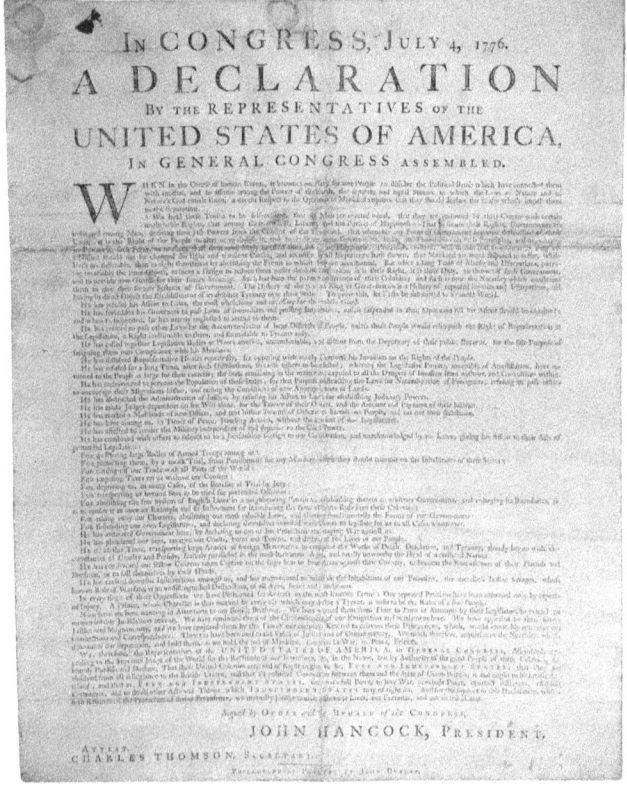

This document represented a new departure in claiming legitimacy on the basis of the rights of man and the sovereignty of the people.

of the ages) – to express the view that a new era was beginning and that past errors and injustices were being left behind. Alexander Hamilton, campaigning for a federal constitution, dismissed 'the history of the petty republics of Greece and Italy', which taught only that they were 'kept in a state of perpetual vibration between the extremes of tyranny and anarchy'. Instead, he argued that modern constitution-makers should turn away from history to the rapidly improving 'science of politics', not least the writings of the French thinker Montesquieu, who argued that large states did not have to be monarchies but could also be federal republics.[43] That said, the constitution of the United States agreed in 1789 by the states that composed it deliberately resurrected the institutions of the Roman republic: the Senate and House of Representatives forming Congress, and a president who would be elected for only four years to guard against despotism.

The French Revolution

Those who made the French Revolution were also torn between drawing legitimacy from Roman history and arguing that rights were derived from nature. The Jacobin revolutionaries, who set up a Republic in 1792 and executed King Louis XVI in 1793, sought legitimacy, as in America, by claiming that they were acting like Roman republicans. They emphasized civic virtue and patriotism, forged against royal tyranny and sustained by the citizen army raised to defend the country and by a civil religion to replace the monarchical Catholic Church. The young revolutionary Saint-Just, urging the Convention parliament to try the king for treason, appealed to Roman precedent: 'Make speed to judge the king because there is not one citizen who does not have the same right over him that Brutus had over Caesar.'[44] 'What is the fundamental principle of democratic and popular government?' asked Jacobin leader Maximilien Robespierre. 'It is virtue, I mean the public virtue that worked so many wonders in Greece and Rome and which will produce even more amazing ones in republican France.'[45]

On the other hand, the revolutionary project was predicated on the idea that sovereignty now came from the people, not from God, and that a new constitution should protect the self-evident rights of man. 'Men are born, and always continue, free and equal in respect of their rights', read the Declaration of the Rights of Man, 'and these rights are liberty, property, security, and resistance of oppression.' It continued: 'The nation is essentially the source of all sovereignty; nor can any individual, or any body of men, be entitled to any authority which is not expressly derived from it.' On this basis, and in short order, a National Assembly was set up; nobility, feudalism and provincial liberties were abolished and the Catholic Church was reformed. In October 1793 a revolutionary calendar was brought in which declared 22 September 1792, the date of the foundation of the Republic, as the start of Year I.

This assertion of a new legitimacy, flying in the face of the tradition and sanctity that upheld monarchy, was anathema to the Whig politician and writer Edmund Burke, who feared that such revolutionary ideas would cross the Channel. His *Reflections on the Revolution in France* (1791) rejected the principles of 1789 in favour of those of the 1688 Revolution in

Britain which, he said, was not really revolutionary but 'made to preserve our ancient indisputable laws and liberties, and that ancient constitution of government which is our only security for law and liberty'. He was horrified by the French National Assembly making up a new constitution from scratch and argued that 'All the reformations we have hitherto made have proceeded upon the principle of reference to antiquity', going back to Magna Carta.[46]

Burke's arguments were in turn rejected by those in Britain who were excited by the French Revolution. The radical Tom Paine, who visited France in its early months, wrote *Rights of Man* (1791) to rebut Burke's appeal to the ancient constitution used to legitimate Britain's monarchical and aristocratic rule. 'I am contending for the rights of the living, and against their being willed away … by the manuscript-assumed authority of the dead', he proclaimed, 'and Mr Burke is contending for the authority of the dead over the rights and freedom of the living.' Ironically, Paine suggested that those who defended antiquity 'do not go far enough into antiquity' and that if they went back to man as was shaped by his maker they would find, as the French and American revolutionaries said, that 'all men are born equal and with equal natural right'.[47]

The descent of the French Revolution into war and terror waged against its enemies provoked a hostile reaction from early historians. The Jesuit Abbé Augustin Barruel, who went into exile in England, wrote *Memoirs Illustrating the History of Jacobinism* (1798–99) which defined a counter-revolutionary position. He argued that the revolution had been caused gratuitously by a conspiracy of Enlightenment philosophes and Freemasons in order to overthrow the Catholic Church, monarchy and the traditional social order.

After the restoration of the monarchy in 1814 and 1815 (with a brief return of Napoleon in between) liberals seeking a middle way between royal absolutism and mob rule sought lessons from the revolution. Journalist and aspiring liberal politician Adolphe Thiers published a *History of the French Revolution* (1823-27) that criticized both the restored absolute monarchy and the 'vile multitude' who had driven the 'excesses' of the revolution. He looked to the constitutional monarchy that functioned in France in 1789–92 as well as to the British monarchy of the Glorious Revolution of 1688 as a model for the constitutional French monarchy of 1830, of which he became a leading minister.

Unfortunately for the likes of Thiers, the restoration of the monarchy had not put to rest those who were still fighting to restore the republic in France. The question was, would the republic bring back the Terror? Jules Michelet, history professor at the Collège de France, said no. His *History of the French Revolution*, published in 1847, asserted that the revolution of 1789, far from being violent and divisive, was 'profoundly pacific' and brought the French people together, providing a road map for the return of a peaceful, democratic republic in 1848.

Unfortunately, the wave of revolutions of 1848, which took Europe by storm, were highly divisive and provoked very different reactions among historians. Thomas Babington Macaulay, a former Indian official, MP and secretary for war, and poet, published the first two parts of his *History of England* in November 1848. The dramatic centrepiece of this work was the acceptance of the crown in 1689 by William of Orange and Mary, having agreed to the Declaration of Right, to huge applause from the London crowd. Macaulay claimed that England was exceptional and avoided revolution in 1848 because it had found a middle way between absolutism and mob rule in 1688. 'It is because we had a preserving revolution in the seventeenth century that we have not had a destroying revolution in the nineteenth', he argued. 'It is because we had freedom in the midst of servitude that we have order in the midst of anarchy.'[48]

Karl Marx, a committed revolutionary, had a very different view of the revolutions of 1848. A native of the Rhineland, which after 1814 was part of the Prussian state, regretted that Germans 'have shared the restorations of modern peoples, without sharing their revolutions. We have had restorations, firstly because other peoples dared to make a revolution, and secondly because other peoples suffered a counter-revolution.'[49] In exile from political persecution in Paris in 1843 and Brussels in 1845, he published *The Communist Manifesto* on the eve of the outbreak of revolution. For Marx, history was not so much a source of legitimacy as a law of development that predicted that proletarian revolution was inevitable. He dovetailed the French history of political revolution with the British history of industrial revolution to argue that as industrialization spread internationally, so proletarian revolution came closer. 'The history of all hitherto existing society is the history of class struggles', he announced. In the French Revolution, he argued, the bourgeoisie overthrew the feudal lords and opened the way for the fast development of industrial capitalism, requiring the greater exploitation of more and more workers. Strikes and protests were the outcome and the Communist Party would emerge as 'the most advanced and resolute section of the working class parties of every country'.[50]

Slavery and the American Civil War

In the United States the Declaration of Rights and the constitution were agreed upon as the source of legitimacy, but they were subject to different interpretations by rival parties. Debates on the constitution were nominally about how much power should rest with the states and how much with the federal government, but they became more intractable because they intersected with the question of slavery.

Tensions between the slave-holding states of the South and non-slave states of the North exploded after the election of Abraham Lincoln in 1860, with each side appealing for justification to the Declaration of Independence and the constitution. Jefferson Davis, the Mississippi senator who became president of the Confederate States in the Civil War, argued that when the Declaration of Independence said that 'all men are created equal' it meant the political community of citizens, excluding slaves, whom slave-owning citizens regarded as their property. He also claimed that the liberties of property-owners and states in the Union were being violated by 'the tyranny of an unbridled majority, the most odious and least responsible form of despotism'.[51] Abraham Lincoln riposted in 1863 by proclaiming the emancipation of four million slaves living in the Confederate States and, after defeating the Confederate army at Gettysburg that year, dedicated a cemetery there by appealing to the Declaration of Independence:

> Four score and seven years ago our fathers brought forth a new nation, conceived in Liberty, and dedicated to the proposition that all men are created equal. Now we are engaged in a great civil war, testing whether that nation, or any nation so conceived and dedicated, can long endure ... we here highly resolve that these dead shall not have died in vain – that this nation, under God, shall have a new birth of freedom – and that government of the people, by the people, for the people, shall not perish from the Earth.[52]

Debates among historians about the origins and meaning of the Civil War were, as in European debates on the French Revolution, shaped by power struggles and the changing historical context. Although the United States lacked a strong Marxist tradition, progressivism from around 1900 sought to bend corporate capitalism to democracy. Progressive historian Charles Beard, who resigned his professorship at Columbia University in 1917 as he found the institution too reactionary, and his suffragist wife Mary, argued in *The Rise of American Civilization* (1927) that the Civil War was a 'social war' and 'Second Revolution' along the lines of the English and French revolutions, 'in which the capitalists, labourers and farmers of the North and West drove from power in the national government the planting aristocracy of the South'.[53]

2.6: The Old South

The Old South is the term given to the southern slave states of the United States of the antebellum era. It was imagined ideally, as a golden age, after it was swept away by the Civil War, the abolition of slavery, and reconstruction. It characterized itself as a rural, hierarchical and Christian society very different from the urban, industrial and individualistic Yankee North. The plantation was seen not as a site of exploitation and cruelty but as a microcosm of harmony in which honourable country gentlemen, chaste southern belles and cheerful, hard-working slaves all knew their place. It has frequently been represented with more than a tinge of romance and nostalgia, most famously in Margaret Mitchell's 1936 novel and the subsequent film, *Gone with the Wind*.

Marginal in the pro-business America of the 1920s, the Beards were criticized by historians, many of them at Northern universities, who defended the way of life of 'the Old South'. Replying two years later, Ulrich Bonnell Phillips of the University of Michigan, argued that the 'peculiar institution' of slavery had in fact civilized the slaves, who had 'no memories of Africa as home'.[54] Indiana journalist and historian Claude Bowers argued that in the so-called Reconstruction era after the Civil War, 'the Southern people were literally put to the torture'.[55] J.G. Randall of the University of Illinois concurred that after the Civil War the Federal army had established a 'semi-military regime' in the South, aided by 'carpetbagging' Northern politicians and 'scalawags' seeking to increase the Black vote, until the South regained control of its destiny when Northern troops were withdrawn in 1877.[56]

In 1963 civil rights campaigner Martin Luther King appealed to Lincoln's Emancipation Proclamation and to the Declaration of Independence in the speech he delivered, symbolically, on the steps of the Lincoln Memorial in Washington:

> One hundred years later we must face the tragic fact that the Negro is still not free. ... When the architects of our republic wrote the magnificent words of the Constitution and the Declaration of Independence they were signing a promissory note to which every American was to fall heir. This note was a promise that all men would be guaranteed the inalienable rights of life, liberty and the pursuit of happiness. It is obvious today that America has defaulted on this promissory note in so far as her citizens of colour are concerned ... I have a dream that one day this nation will rise up and live out the meaning of its creed; 'We hold these truths to be self-evident: that all men are created equal.'[57]

Figure 2.5: From *Scenes on a Cotton Plantation*, sketched by A.R. Waud (*Harper's Weekly*, 1867), wood engraving (detail)

This peaceful image of a plantation, and many others like it, sanitized slavery and conveyed a myth of a harmonious Old South.

The civil rights era opened the door to a new generation of progressive historians, who denounced both slavery and the system of segregation and white supremacy that was imposed in the South by the so-called Jim Crow laws (the system of legalized racial segregation that existed in the South) after 1876. Kenneth Stampp, a history professor at Berkeley, California, took up the euphemism of 'the peculiar institution' in 1956 to reject in the name of equality the Southern notion that 'some men are born with saddles on their back and others booted and spurred to ride them'.[58] In 1965 he defended the Reconstruction government which had defended the civil and political rights of African Americans as 'the most democratic the South had ever known'.[59] Eric Foner, a younger professor at Columbia, whose Jewish-Communist teacher parents had been dismissed in the McCarthy era and who threw himself into the civil rights movement, argued in *Free Soil, Free Labour, Free Men* that the Northern Republicans had been motivated in the Civil War by a coherent ideology of emancipation and social progress.

This interpretation became the new orthodoxy, but historians of the South retaliated after the Reagan era. Gary Gallagher secured a professorship at the University of Virginia in 1998 by suggesting that the 'lost cause' of the Confederacy powerfully redefined the Southern identity. Meanwhile Karen Cox of the University of North Carolina showed how popular culture had developed the myth of a 'romantic, pre-modern South', typified by the 1939 film *Gone with the Wind*, that even Northerners could enjoy.[60]

The Russian Revolution and the Cold War

The French Revolution in its drama and reach became the inspiration for all subsequent revolutionaries. It demonstrated what could be done by determined revolutionaries and also provided a new legitimacy. Importantly, too, it offered lessons in what to do and what not to do. Thermidor, the revolutionary month in Year II (July 1794), when Robespierre was overthrown, was a cautionary tale for radicals but an inspiration for moderates. Brumaire, the revolutionary month in Year VII (November 1799) when Napoleon Bonaparte seized power and declared that the revolution was over, was a nightmare for all revolutionaries.

As he switched between being a revolutionary and writing about revolution, Marx offered historical interpretations in real time. When the French Second Republic was overthrown by Napoleon Bonaparte's nephew, Louis Napoleon, on 2 December 1851, he conceded in *The Eighteenth Brumaire of Louis Bonaparte* (1852) that the direction taken by history was not always a straight line. History occurs twice, he said, 'the first time as tragedy, the second as farce'. He defined Bonapartism as a regime in which the state had made itself independent of all classes and dismissed Louis Napoleon, who became Napoleon III, as 'an adventurer blown in from abroad, raised on the shield by a drunken soldiery, which he has bought with liquor and sausages, and which he must constantly ply with sausage anew'.[61] After Napoleon III's defeat in 1870 at the hands of the Prussians, however, Marx argued that the road to revolution was rejoined. In *The Civil War in France* he welcomed the Paris Commune as the first working-class government which, though soon crushed by the forces of bourgeois reaction aided by Bismarck's army of occupation, was 'the glorious harbinger of a new society'.[62]

Russian revolutionary Lenin took up Marx's point that the party would act as a revolutionary vanguard, bringing political consciousness and organization to all classes of the population, peasants as well as workers.[63] The Bolshevik Party was conceived as a communist version of the Jacobins, and Lenin's rival Martov ironically called him 'Robespierre'.[64] After the fall of the Tsarist regime in February 1917, Lenin looked for inspiration from the Paris Commune, while also seeking to learn lessons from its failure. Although, he argued, it had abolished the bourgeois bureaucracy, police and standing army in the capital, it had not replaced these with a dictatorship of the proletariat and was thus overwhelmed by a White Terror of its enemies.[65] He had therefore no qualms about using Red Terror against counter-revolutionaries.

Histories of this extraordinary event were quick to be written by journalists. John Reed, who was in Petrograd for the October Revolution, wrote an enthusiastic *Ten Days that Shook the World* and managed to obtain an endorsement from Lenin himself for 'the workers of the world'.[66] William Chamberlin, who went to Moscow in 1921, wrote *The Russian Revolution*, which portrayed Lenin as a 'supreme genius of revolutionary leadership' and praised the ambition of the Bolsheviks 'building socialism' in a 'backward, semi-Asiatic peasant country'.[67] Chamberlin left the Soviet Union in 1934, by which time Joseph Stalin, the new general secretary of the party, had turned the dictatorship of the proletariat into a dictatorship of the party over the proletariat and embarked on purging his enemies. Chamberlin was shocked by Stalin's purges and the use of famine as an 'instrument of national policy' against peasants refusing to move to the 'slavery' of collective farms.[68]

The history of the French Revolution and Marx's interpretation of it were weaponized to contest the betrayal of the early promise of the Russian Revolution by Stalin. Lenin's former comrade-in-arms Trotsky denounced Stalin's betrayal as both Thermidor – 'the triumph of the bureaucracy over the masses' – and Bonapartism. 'The Stalin regime', he wrote in 1936, 'rising above a politically atomized society, resting upon a police and officers' corps and allowing no control whatever, is obviously a variation of Bonapartism'.[69] Stalin, meanwhile, reached for monarchical legitimacy. He compared himself to the first tsar of all Russia, Ivan the Terrible, and his purges to Ivan's massacre of the Russian boyars (feudal nobility). Film director Sergei Eisenstein brought out the first part of *Ivan the Terrible* as a tribute in 1944, but Stalin forbade the release of part two. 'Your tsar is indecisive,' he complained, 'he resembles Hamlet. Ivan the Terrible was very cruel. You can show he was cruel. But you must show why he *needed to be cruel*.'[70]

Historians of the Russian Revolution disagreed about how to interpret it. Some saw it as the new beacon of revolution, replacing the French model, others as a brutal dictatorship. E.H. Carr, who worked for the Foreign Office and the League of Nations in the interwar period and visited the Soviet Union in 1937, was convinced that the Soviet planned economy was the best answer to the near-collapse of capitalism in the 1930s and published an admiring multi-volume account of the Soviet Union between 1950 and 1978, never actually getting into the dark years of the 1930s.

As the Second World War gave way to the Cold War, E.H. Carr was left out on a limb. Hostility to Stalin and Stalinism, especially for the purges, became the order of the day. Zbigniew Brzezinski, the son of a Polish diplomat, published his Harvard PhD in 1956 as *The Permanent Purge*, describing Stalin's policy as an instrument of totalitarianism, and in 1976 became Jimmy Carter's National Security Advisor. Robert Conquest, who worked for the British Foreign Office after the war and then at Stanford University's Hoover Institution, published *The Great Terror* in 1968. He distinguished the 'fanatical idealists' of the Jacobin Terror from the 'vulgar crime' and 'frightful slaughter' of Stalin's, estimating there had been a million executions and three million deaths in the labour camps.[71] This viewpoint was reinforced by the Soviet dissident Roy Medvedev, who denounced Stalin's 'lust for power' and 'cruelty and viciousness' in a 1972 work, *Let History Judge*, that he could only publish abroad.[72]

Debates about Marxism and the Russian Revolution had an impact on how historians thought about the English Civil War and French Revolution. Christopher Hill, who visited the Soviet Union in 1934 and secretly joined the Communist Party, presented the Civil War in 1940 as *The English Revolution*. He argued trenchantly that 'the Civil War was a class war in which the despotism of Charles I was defended by reactionary forces of the established Church and conservative landlords'.[73] According to Hill, the revolutionary period of 1649–60 unleashed republicans, democrats, religious radicals and even early communists. His anti-communist contemporary and rival, Hugh Trevor-Roper, meanwhile, described Macaulay as 'unquestionably the greatest of the "whig historians"', and adopted Whig history himself. He saw the Civil War as a struggle between country gentry and a corrupt court but was unable to complete a major history of it he began in 1957. He disliked the idea of revolution that Hill embraced and 'the grim, repellent face of middle-class English Puritanism' but was unable to put anything in its place.[74] Meanwhile the Tory interpretation pioneered by Lord Clarendon was taken up by Veronica Wedgwood who, like him, titled her two-volume account of the Civil War *The Great Rebellion* (1955–58). She denounced the claims of parliament and the army and saw Charles I not as an absolutist but 'the defender of his subjects' liberties and the laws of the land against arbitrary power'.[75]

Similar debates about Marxism and the Russian Revolution also divided French historians in the lead-up to the bicentenary of the French Revolution in 1989. This was in the context of Russia's Thermidor in 1985, when Mikhail Gorbachev became general secretary of the party and for the sake of economic development demanded its democratization and its opening to new ideas. Naturally, he did not call it Thermidor, but claimed legitimacy from Lenin's 'war on bureaucratic practices' and ridicule of 'mere memorising and repetition of formulas'.[76]

As these changes occurred in the Soviet Union, the Marxist and communist interpretation of the French Revolution, which held that it was a class war and that Bolshevism was a reincarnation of Jacobinism, began to lose its hegemony in France. Anti-Marxist historians now mounted attacks on the Marxist orthodoxy. In 1985 a thesis on the Vendée, which rose in defence of

2.7: Marxist history

Marxist history was an approach developed by Marx and his disciples, which was dominant between the 1848 revolutions and the last third of the twentieth century. It postulated that economic factors determined social and political developments and conflicts. Marxist theory held that people were above all producers but that the 'means of production' (land, capital) were owned by a few, who were able to exploit them. It argued that in any society this economic 'substructure' conditioned the political and ideological 'superstructure'. It postulated that the rapidly changing capitalist 'forces of production' (widening markets, the division of labour, mechanization) would come into conflict with feudal 'relations of production' (serfdom, guilds) and provoke bourgeois revolution. Capital would expand by increasing the size and exploitation of the proletariat and socialist revolution would follow. Marxist history sought to discover these theoretical developments in existing societies in order to build socialist and communist parties that would harness them to take power. Not all Marxist historians were communists, but the collapse of communism had a negative effect on Marxist history.

church and king in 1793 and was brutally suppressed in the Terror, was presented at the Sorbonne and published under the provocative title, *The Franco-French Genocide*.[77] Then, former communist and now anti-communist historian François Furet led a revisionist attack which praised the beginning of the revolution in 1789 while demonizing the Terror and argued that in France the revolution (communism) was now over. The country, he said, had left behind its violent past to become a card-carrying Western liberal democracy.[78]

Back in Russia, the dissolution of the Soviet Union in 1991 and end of its Communist Party meant that Marxism and Leninism ceased to be invoked as a source of political legitimacy. On the contrary, Vladimir Putin, who became president of Russia in 2000, attacked Lenin for founding a Soviet Union that allowed states to secede and put a 'time bomb under the edifice of our statehood'. He did not pay tribute to Stalin because the legacy of the purges had not been digested and instead resurrected the cult of tsarist Russia, especially of Alexander III with his 'righteous and unshakeable firmness' and Nicholas II's prime minister after the 1905 Revolution, Pyotr Stolypin, with his ambition to prevent revolution breaking out again and restore Russia's status as a great power.[79]

China

In China, the legitimacy of the Mandate of Heaven remained more or less intact until the fall of the Qing dynasty, China's last, in 1911. Revolutionaries were inspired by both the French and Russian revolutions, but coming later they had the advantage of learning more carefully from previous mistakes in order to keep the Chinese Communist Party in power.

As the Qing dynasty and Chinese society reeled under impact of the Opium Wars after 1842, a new leader and convert to Christianity, Hung Hsiu-ch'uan, founded a Society of God-Worshippers in Nanjing and launched the Taiping rebellion in 1850. Significantly, he played on the Mandate of Heaven by calling himself the Heavenly King of a Heavenly Kingdom of Eternal Peace and Prosperity. The Qing regained control, but following the country's defeat by Japan in 1895, the dynasty was in trouble again. Young revolutionaries gathered in exile in Tokyo and published *Minbao*, the People's Newspaper. One of them, Wang Dong, tried to reconcile the Mandate of Heaven and revolution by arguing that 'since heaven can no longer see nor hear, the people would act to heaven's desire'. Another, Sun Yat-sen, formed a revolutionary Revive China Society in exile in 1905, which unambiguously adopted the French principles of Liberty, Equality and Universal Brotherhood.

The May Fourth movement of 1919, in protest at China's further humiliation at the Versailles Peace conference, blew away the cobwebs of Confucianism. New ideas abounded as the country descended into chaos, ruled by regional warlords. Sun Yat-sen's Guomindang, or Nationalist Party, was now rivalled by a fledgling Communist Party. In 1920–21 a team of young Chinese communists, among them Deng Xiaoping, went to work and study in France, since one of its organizers, Mao Zedong, argued that 'France is the exemplar of a political revolution and Russia is an exemplar of a social revolution'.[80] For a while, the

Guomindang and the Communists worked together to defeat the warlords and establish the Chinese Republic, but in 1926 the Guomindang's new leader, Chiang Kai-shek, suppressed his communist allies. Like Marx and Lenin, Mao now turned to the Paris Commune for inspiration. He saw this as the first revolution of the working class but, echoing Lenin, thought that it was defeated because 'there was no united, centralized and disciplined party' and that it was 'too merciful' to its enemies and thus suffered a 'white terror' that killed 100,000 people. 'If we do not inflict a mortal blow on the enemy', he concluded, 'the enemy will inflict a mortal blow on us.'[81]

Whereas the Bolsheviks had seized power very suddenly in 1917, the Chinese Communists fought a 28-year revolution before taking power in 1949. Mao's main concern was to maintain the momentum of the revolution to avoid a Chinese Thermidor. Having gained power, he collectivized the economy and in 1966 declared a Cultural Revolution to purge all pre- and anti-revolutionary ideas. Given his reading of Marx, Mao was delighted by the proclamation of a Commune in Shanghai, but then feared that the whole country might 'escape the party's control and become "the People's Commune of China"'.

As far as China was concerned, there was initial enthusiasm for the Cultural Revolution among many Western intellectuals, who were opposed to American imperialism in Vietnam and saw Mao's communism in the 1960s as a liberating alternative to Western communism, which they regarded as still in the

Stalinist mould. Mao's slogans – 'a revolution is not a dinner party' and 'it is right to rebel' – fired up a generation of Maoist youth. Cambridge economist Joan Robinson, who visited China in 1967, was excited that 'large numbers of revolutionary young people, previously unknown, have become courageous and daring pathbreakers'.[82] American academics William Hinton and Stuart Schram, who had both been persecuted during the anti-communist McCarthy era in the Cold War United States, were equally positive. Hinton praised Mao for 'mobilizing the mass movement when this was the key to the future and then guiding it through one crisis after another'.[83] Schram approved 'struggle meetings' organized by the Red Guard in which class enemies were taught the error of their ways because 'struggle means destruction and transformation means establishing something new'.[84]

After Mao's death in 1976, leadership passed to Deng Xiaoping, who ushered in an economic Thermidor, criticized the Cultural Revolution as 'disastrous for us' and admitted that 'Comrade Mao was not infallible'. He was nevertheless horrified at the way in which Gorbachev's reforms were weakening the Soviet Union and refused the political Thermidor demanded by young demonstrators, who in the spring of 1989 erected a statue of the Goddess of Democracy, copying the Statue of Liberty, in Beijing's Tiananmen Square. The police and army were sent in and killed at least a thousand demonstrators, who were accused of launching a 'counter-revolutionary rebellion' to

2.8: The Chinese Cultural Revolution

An existential question faced by revolutionaries has long been: what should they do after they take power? In the Soviet Union they set up a dictatorship of the party bureaucracy. In China, Mao Zedong sought to avoid this in 1966 by announcing continuous revolution, a class struggle aimed at an emerging party bureaucracy and his political rivals. It was carried through by proletarian youth enrolled into the Red Guards, who were encouraged to wage war on the 'four olds' – ideas, culture, habits and custom. This involved mass meetings in universities, the streets, factories and villages to ritually humiliate party cadres and intellectuals accused of bourgeois or counter-revolutionary deviation. Meetings sometimes degenerated into beatings and killing. Power was seized from below and in Shanghai a commune was set up, modelled on the Paris Commune. Mao was forced to bring in the Red Army to restore order. The events in China inspired a generation of young Maoists worldwide, who delighted in this anti-Stalinist version of Marxism and 'went to the people' in the factories and farms. In France they played a leading role in 1968. Later information about the degree of violence in China caused the same young Maoists to denounce the Cultural Revolution.

'establish a bourgeois republic, an out-and-out vassal of the West'.[85]

At the same time, after Mao's death, Western intellectuals and academics changed their attitude to the Cultural Revolution, even though they had praised

Figure 2.6: 'Struggle session' at Tsinghua University High School, May 1966

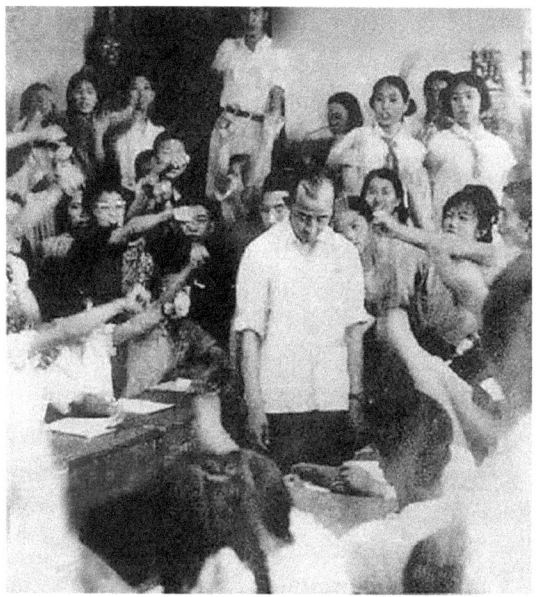

This photograph of a 'struggle session' shows a Chinese school principal, Wan Bangru, being humiliated early in the Cultural Revolution. Images like these served to discredit the Chinese Revolution in the West.

it only a few years earlier. French students Jacques and Claudie Broyelle, who had visited China in 1966 and returned to Paris to found a Maoist movement amid the protests of 1968, returned to China in the 1970s. They now denounced struggle sessions, which involved public criticism and humiliation, as 'the pillory' and judged that 'the Chinese system of preventive detention and camps is recognizably descended from the Soviet system'.[86] American academic Anne Thurston, who collected testimony in China in 1981–82, suggested that 'China's Great Proletarian Cultural Revolution is surpassed only by the Nazi Holocaust, the Stalinist purges and the recent genocide in Cambodia'.[87]

After the Tiananmen Square massacre, Chinese dissidents keen to criticize the Communist system added their voices to the clamour. Novelist Zheng Yi returned to Guangxi province, where he had been a Red Guard, and unearthed evidence of the killings of thousands of class enemies in struggle meetings which had been followed by cannibalism.[88] These stories of massacre and cannibalism were taken up by Swedish Sinologist Michael Schoenhals, who then fed them into the mainstream of Harvard's Fairbank Center, where the province was described as 'the juvenile state of nature, foreshadowed in microcosm by Nobel-prize-winning novelist William Golding in *Lord of the Flies*'.[89]

The Chinese Communist Party held on to power by entering its own Bonapartist phase. Xi Jinping, elected general secretary in 2012 and president of China in 2013, persuaded the 13th National People's Congress in 2018 to allow him to become president for life, as Napoleon Bonaparte became Consul for life in 1802. Even before that, however, on a state visit to Paris in 2014, Xi let slip that he might become emperor: 'Napoleon said that China is a sleeping lion and, when she awakes, the world will shake. The lion of China has already awakened', he said and then, as if to reassure his audience, 'this is a peaceful, pleasant and civilised lion'.[90] Moreover, in May 2023, when Xi Jinping hosted the five presidents of the Central Asian republics at a summit in the ancient Chinese capital of Xi'an, he was accused on social media of behaving like a Chinese emperor receiving western 'barbarians'.[91]

The struggle for power is at the heart of history. Those who take power and exercise it have to demonstrate that they do so legitimately, and that legitimacy is underwritten by history. They are emperor of a dynasty that has been consecrated by the Mandate of Heaven or divine right. They are king because they overthrew a tyrant who had forfeited the right to rule. Following revolution, they are democratic leaders who embody the sovereignty of the people and are sanctioned by the revolutionary tradition. They are overthrown because they have betrayed the revolutionary principles of the rights of man through terror or coup d'état.

Historians are themselves at the centre of this debate. They may sit in university libraries away from the cut and thrust of power, but rarely do they escape the power implications of their work. Some historians have served as court historians or official historians, tasked with defending a leader or political party. Others write scholarly books and articles about ancient Rome, medieval kingship, the English Civil War or the French Revolution, but find it difficult to escape the political debates at the heart of them. With other subjects, such as the American Civil War or civil rights or recent Russian or Chinese history, questions of power and legitimacy are inescapable. The changing historical contexts alter the nature of the debate. The English and French revolutions had to be reassessed after the Russian Revolution, Napoleon was reassessed in the light of Hitler, and the American Civil War was reassessed after the civil rights movement. Historians, moreover, are engaged in ongoing historical and thus political debate. It is not possible to reconcile the interpretations of Christopher Hill and Hugh Trevor-Roper, as a school contemporary of mine tried to do, nor those of E.H. Carr and Robert Conquest. As for Napoleon, we have only to turn to Dutch historian Pieter Geyl's 1949 study, *Napoleon: For and Against*.[92]

Whose history is it anyway? History and identity

It is a truism that history is written by the victors. The documents we find in the archives are created by rulers, bureaucracies and churches. The histories we read are generally written either by academics whose work has been reviewed by other academics or by professional writers whose literary talents are favoured by agents and publishers who shape the market. They may be close to those in power and write about people who wield power. Outside the magic circle are those who have been marginalized, suppressed, excluded or silenced. If they ever had records, these have been lost or destroyed. If they wrote histories, these may not have been published or have been dismissed. Those without power lack a voice, or else their voice is not heard.

There is nevertheless a saying from one of those groups that was defeated and excluded, the North American Sioux people, that 'A people without a history is like a wind upon the buffalo grass'. The message is that those without a history have no identity. Nothing is known about who they are, where they come from and what they wish to say. Without a history, a group not only lacks identity but has no agency in the world. It cannot make claims for itself against those who exercise power, let alone wrest power from them. It may be that excluded groups have a voice in terms of an oral tradition, in the form of songs, ballads, sagas and legends. But these are stories that they tell to themselves, not to anyone else.

Here we will explore the history-writing of a selection of groups that have long been excluded and silenced: workers, women, LGBTQ+ minorities and Black minorities. Each in turn has fought to define an identity and to make claims on the basis of that identity. For this to happen they have had to write their own history. Three phases are clear. In the first phase some of those workers, women, LGBTQ+ and Black minorities told their own story, generally a story of suffering, struggle and exclusion, which linked their own lives to the wider experience of the group seeking to define itself. In a second phase their stories were recognized by academic historians, and some of the activists themselves found positions in the academy. New historical disciplines were invented: the history of labour, the history of women, the history of enslaved, immigrant and Indigenous peoples, and university curricula were modified in order to make space for these histories alongside the conventional histories of upper- and middle-class white men. This, however, has frequently led to a third phase, an often bitter push-back by those who claimed that their own histories risked being marginalized, suppressed or excluded. At stake was the question of whose history was going to be victorious or dominant among the competing histories of different groups, and which was going to remain or become sidelined.

What about the workers? Escaping 'the enormous condescension of posterity'

The existence of an urban, industrial working class was 'discovered' in the early nineteenth century by middle-class professionals whose capitalist brothers had called the class into being to work in their factories, but who posed social challenges of poverty, ill-health, criminality and, potentially, riot and rebellion. In 1832, for example, James Kay-Shuttleworth published *The Moral and Physical Condition of the Working Classes employed in the Cotton Manufacture of Manchester*, in which he likened the workers, many of them of Irish origin, to 'savage tribes'.[93] Ten years later the same Manchester population was observed by Friedrich Engels, who was sent by his German manufacturer father to work in the offices of a mill he owned in Salford but who, having met Karl Marx, drew the more portentous conclusions that 'in England a social war is already being waged' and 'the whole working class is behind the great Chartist assault on their oppressors'.[94]

In time, some of those workers began to write their own stories, highlighting their struggles with hardship, poverty and prison, linking them to the story of the struggles of the working class for emancipation in the face of brutal repression. William Lovett, the son of a Cornish fisherman who was drowned before William was born, went to London to work as a cabinet-maker, and was one of the founders of the London Working Men's Association. He helped draw up the People's Charter of 1838, demanding the vote for working people, and was imprisoned for seditious libel in 1840. In 1876, the year before he died, he published *The Life and Struggles of William Lovett in his Pursuit of Bread, Knowledge and Freedom*, a history of the Chartist movement and his role in it.

In France, histories by workers and revolutionaries were transformed by the outbreak – and even more by the brutal suppression – of the Paris Commune in 1871. In 1876 Prosper-Olivier Lissagaray, who fled to London for his life, published a first *History of the Commune* with the help of Marx's daughter Eleanor, with whom he had a relationship and who translated it into English in 1886. He heaped scorn on the 'rage of the bourgeoisie' and its vengeful army which, he calculated, had killed 25,000 men, women and children during the Bloody Week of late May 1871.[95] Louise Michel, a schoolteacher who was involved with the Commune in the Montmartre district, published her memoirs in 1886. These were very much a tribute to her lover, Théophile Ferré, who was executed by firing squad for his leading role in the Commune, and whose last words were: 'I entrust my memory and my vengeance to the future.'[96] Such accounts forged the history that defined the struggles of the French and (as we have seen) the international working class.

2.9: The Paris Commune

The Paris Commune was a revolutionary government that ruled Paris for ten weeks in the spring of 1871 in the aftermath of the Franco-Prussian war. Insurrection was triggered on 18 March when the republican Government of National Defence, which had decamped to Bordeaux, made an armistice with the Prussians occupying much of the country and tried to disband the National Guard, which had been defending Paris that winter during a Prussian siege. A Commune was elected on 22 March from the city's districts, revolutionary clubs and National Guardsmen, and from this a Committee of Public Safety formed. There was little time to push through revolutionary measures. The Government of National Defence, which now moved to Versailles, sent in an army to crush the Commune. The Communards executed hostages, but the Versailles forces killed about ten thousand Parisians in fighting and another ten thousand by summary execution during the so-called 'Bloody Week' of 21–28 May 1871. The Commune inspired Marx, Lenin and Mao Zedong as a working-class government (which it was only in part), while its martyrs inspired later socialist and communist movements in France and elsewhere.

Workers in Germany were torn between a trade union movement that became increasingly effective and an authoritarian state which came down brutally on socialism. August Bebel wrote *My Life* in 1912 when his Social Democratic Party was the largest party in

Figure 2.7: Fighting in Père Lachaise cemetery, Paris, 1871 (from *Mémorial Illustré des Deux Sièges de Paris, 1870–1871*)

During the 'Bloody Week' in May 1871 which brought an end to the Paris Commune, government forces brutally suppressed the uprising, killing and executing thousands of Commune soldiers. The rout shown here in Paris's Père Lachaise cemetery and subsequent summary executions helped to build the identity and legitimacy of socialist and communist movements.

the Reichstag but enjoyed no power because of the authoritarian and aristocratic nature of the imperial constitution. He began with his impoverished childhood as an orphan, and described his apprenticeship as a wood-turner, his role in building the labour movement and the party, but also his imprisonment for opposing the war of 1870 and defending the record of the Paris Commune. 'If it did commit acts of violence', he wrote, 'the monarchical governments of Europe have committed acts a hundred times more violent.'[97]

The struggles of the working class in the United States were often promoted by migrants from Europe and were in their image. Samuel Gompers came from a Dutch-Jewish family which emigrated in 1863 when he was 13 from London's East End to New York. 'In the early "seventies"', he recalled, 'New York looked like Paris during the Commune', as he had heard it reported, flooded by politicised refugees from every European country and agitated by labour unrest. He followed his father into the cigar-making trade, joined a union and went on strike in 1877 as unemployment bit and wages were cut. Penniless, he had almost to force a doctor to attend his wife in childbirth. 'Although we did not win', he reflected, 'we learned the fundamentals and techniques which assured success later.'[98] He went on to become the president of the American Federation of Organized Trades and Labor Unions, campaigning successfully for an eight-hour day.

Back in Britain, Will Thorne recalled in *My Life's Battles* his early life in Birmingham as the son of a brickmaker who died when Will was seven, and his own toil in the brickworks, 'being slowly killed' by dust. He moved on to an ammunition factory and Saltley gasworks before he walked to London to work as a stoker in the Old Kent Road gasworks. He read about socialism, met Eleanor Marx and Edward Aveling, joined the Social Democratic Federation and remarked that 'out of evil comes good'. He helped found the Union of Gas Workers and General Labourers, a beacon of the 'new unionism' of less skilled workers, which launched strike action in 1889. He declared it 'A great fight. One of the greatest in the history of the working class in Great Britain.'[99]

The battles of the working class against employers and the state were charted not only by labour activists telling their own stories but by historians of the labour movement with a wider perspective. These historians were generally middle class, but they were socialists or, later, communists who subscribed to Marx's idea that the working class was the bearer of social progress towards a more just society. The first historians of labour and socialism were not necessarily academics, and the joint role of husband-and-wife historians was striking. Later historians were increasingly academics, who fought to establish the history of labour as an academic discipline alongside the traditional history of kings, queens and elites. But the history of labour remained close to the labour movement through organizations such as the Workers' Educational Association (WEA) and labour journals with local roots.

The histories of Sidney and Beatrice Webb derived from their involvement in the Fabian Society of socialist intellectuals, founded in 1884. Beatrice Webb, the daughter of a businessman, researched for her cousin Charles Booth's *Life and Labour of the People in London* and discovered trade unions after the strikes of 1889. 'He has the historic sense', she said of Sidney, who sat with the Progressive majority on the new London County Council.[100] In order to understand and legitimate trade unions they published *The History of Trade Unionism* in 1894, tracing their struggles back to the seventeenth century. Meanwhile through a donation to the Fabian Society they were co-founders in 1895 of the London School of Economics (LSE), which became a hub of economic and social history.

Fifteen years younger than the Webbs, Lawrence and Barbara Hammond were both children of clergymen who, after graduating in classics from Oxford University, embarked on the histories of the *Village Labourer* (1911), which culminated in the labourers' revolt of 1830, and the *Town Labourer* (1917), which indicted the 'modern slavery' of industrial wage-labour. Thirty years younger than the Webbs and criticising them for their cerebral aim of saving labour through organization was Douglas (G.D.H.) Cole, who both pursued an academic career at Oxford and was a leading light on the left of the Labour Party. *The World of Labour*, published in 1913, took into account not only British trade unionism but French syndicalism, which was committed to the strategy of the general strike. Margaret Postgate, converted to pacifism and socialism by her brother Raymond's imprisonment as a conscientious objector in 1916, married Cole in 1918. They both supported the General Strike of 1926 and then spread the gospel of trade unionism and socialism through the WEA. Douglas then collaborated with Raymond Postgate on *The Common People, 1746–1938*, later updated to 1946, which put the struggles of working people for freedom and equality at the heart of English history.

After the Second World War the group of British historians affiliated to the Communist Party Historians' Group made a bid to move the history of the working class into the mainstream of research and teaching. Christopher Hill joined forces with Eric Hobsbawm, who had been educated in Vienna, Berlin and Cambridge before lecturing at Birkbeck College, London; with E.P. Thompson, the son of Methodist missionaries and lecturer at the University of Leeds; and with Raphael Samuel, who taught working people returning to education at Ruskin College Oxford. They launched *Past & Present* journal in 1952 to bring together international research on labour, labour movements and revolution. Hobsbawm published *The Age of Revolution, 1789–1848* in 1962 but the biggest splash was made by E.P. Thompson's *The Making of the English Working Class* in 1963. This explored the complexities of class formation and the forging of a radical intellectual culture among English working people. 'I am seeking', he said, chiding those who dominated history-writing in the universities and literary world, 'to rescue the poor stockinger, the Luddite cropper, the "obsolete" hand-loom weaver, the "utopian" artisan, and even the deluded follower of [the Devon prophetess] Joanna Southcott, from the enormous condescension of posterity.'[101]

In France the pioneering historian of socialism was academic and politician Jean Jaurès. Converted to socialism by defending the striking miners of Carmaux, and elected deputy for that region the following year, he embarked on *A Socialist History of the French Revolution*, of which the first volumes appeared in 1901–04. This argued, following Marx, that the French Revolution was bourgeois, but that its Declaration of Rights of Man and revolutionary democracy were later taken up by democratic socialists to emancipate the working class. A new edition was brought out in 1969 by communist historian Albert Soboul, who had published *The Paris Sans-Culottes of the Year II* in 1958. For a long time, socialist and communist historians focused on the French Revolution rather than later developments. Ernest Labrousse, professor of economic and social history at the Sorbonne from 1947, wrote theses in 1932 and 1943 on the economic origins of the French Revolution. A significant shift, however, came in 1960. That year Jean Maitron, a teacher committed to the labour movement and founder in 1949 of the French Institute of Social History, launched the journal *Le Mouvement Social*. This brought together a cluster of younger communist or socialist historians who were working on labour in the nineteenth century. One of those, Labrousse's student Michelle Perrot, published her thesis, *Workers on Strike, 1871–1890*, in 1972.

In the Federal Republic of Germany, the Bielefeld school of history led by Hans-Ulrich Wehler and Jürgen Kocka was not specifically dedicated to the working class but analysed social structures and developments. By contrast, the German Democratic Republic was deeply invested in the history of the labour movement and communism as its founding myth. In 1966 the Marxist–Leninist Institute of the Central Committee of the Socialist Unity (Communist) Party published a *History of the German Working Class*, while an International Conference of Labour History, launched in Linz in 1964, provided dialogue between labour historians of East and West.

The highpoint of labour history was reached in the 1960s and early 1970s. In Britain, the North-East Labour History Society was set up in 1967, and societies for Scottish and Welsh labour history three years later. After that, however, it began to lose its place in the sun. For over a hundred years it had been carried on the shoulders of an organized labour movement and Marxist historical analysis. But from the late 1970s, organized labour was broken by global finance capital and neoliberalism and their drive for free markets, privatization and a 'flexible' labour force. The defeat of the 1984–85 miners' strike in the UK and deindustrialization swept trade unions aside. Marxism was undermined by the collapse of communist regimes after 1989 and a loss of faith in Marxist thought as an explanatory method. In his 1978 Marx Memorial Lecture on 'The Forward March of Labour Halted?', Eric Hobsbawm bemoaned that this march had already ended, while his *Age of Extremes: The Short Twentieth Century, 1914–1991* (1994) brought history to a close with the collapse of the Soviet Union.

Class, with its emphasis on male waged labour, was no longer a fundamental category of analysis for historians. It was replaced by a much more fluid 'history from below', which included the history of all marginalized groups, including women. In Britain this was characterized by the History Workshop movement developed in Oxford by Raphael Samuel with the launch in 1976 of *History Workshop Journal*. In France it was reflected in Michel de Certeau's *The Practice of Everyday Life* (1984) and in Germany by the setting up of history workshops in Berlin and Alf Lüdtke's *History of Everyday Life* (1995). Moreover, the advent of a more cultural approach to history undermined the Marxist view that economic issues were the driving force of history. Gareth Stedman Jones' pathbreaking article on 'Rethinking Chartism' in *Languages of Class* (1983) argued that Chartist thinking did not simply reflect the economic grievances of the working class but drew on a long tradition of radical thinking going back to the seventeenth century. 'The people' became a much more seductive category than class, as suggested by Selina Todd's *The People: The Rise and Fall of the Working Class, 1910–2010* (2014).

Women and gender: the pen in their hands

'Men have had every advantage of us in telling their own story', says the heroine Anne Elliott in Jane Austen's last novel, *Persuasion*. 'Education has been theirs to a much higher degree; the pen has been in their hands.'[102] Women not only wielded the pen much less, but if they did, they generally disguised their identity, lest they be criticized for breaking into a public sphere that was not theirs. Jane Austen did not sign her novels but presented herself only as 'A Lady'. Other nineteenth-century women writers adopted men's names; Mary Ann Evans called herself George Eliot, while Amantine Aurore Lucile Dupin called herself George Sand. Louise Michel, heroine of the Paris Commune whom we met in the previous section, confessed that she did not want to write her memoirs: 'I felt a repugnance to talk about myself that one might feel if I undressed in public.' Fortunately, she did eventually write them, and pithily declared that 'Were the equality between the sexes to be recognised it would be a wonderful breach in human stupidity.'[103]

Louise Michel made a breach in human stupidity both as a revolutionary and as a woman. Others came to revolution through their fight for women's rights and were keen to legitimate their claims by reference to history. Suffragette leader Emmeline Pankhurst's earliest memory was raising money for America's newly emancipated slaves. Her 'Votes for Women' movement began in 1906 by petitioning parliament, and denounced the resurrection of a law of Charles II against 'tumultuous petitions' to stop them. She laid claim to 'the ancient constitutional right of petition, secured to the people by the Bill of Rights, and cherished by uncounted generations of Englishmen'. After the police brutality used against women on 'Black Friday', 18 November 1910, she announced a Women's Revolution. 'If it is right for men to fight for their freedom, and God knows what the human race would be like today if men had not, then it is right for women to fight for their freedom and the freedom of the children they bear.'[104]

Feminists fighting for emancipation often traced history back to much earlier times in order to justify their claims. This analysis owed much to Engels' *Origins of the Family, Private Property and the State*

Figure 2.8: A suffragette arrested in the street in London, 1914

Women struggling for their rights needed to write their own history in defence of their claims.

(1884), which postulated that 'savage' societies were matriarchal but that the invention of private property in 'civilized' societies introduced monogamy so that fathers could be sure that the male heirs to whom they were passing their property were their own. Simone de Beauvoir used this argument in *The Second Sex* (1949), which became second-wave feminists' bible in the 1960s and 1970s. Nomadic societies which worshipped Mother Earth, she agreed, were matriarchal, but women were 'dethroned by the advent of private property' and were reduced to private property themselves, bought and sold like cattle or slaves.[105] One of those second-wave feminists was Juliet Mitchell, a young university teacher of English and a New Left campaigner. Her 1966 article, 'Women: The Longest Revolution' (later published as a book), took up the analyses of Engels and De Beauvoir to demand not only that women be granted equal work and equal education but also that the monogamous family be replaced by much more diverse 'intersexual and intergenerational relationships', including same-sex couples.[106]

Historical arguments with a shorter time frame were used by American feminists. Betty Friedan published *The Feminine Mystique* (1963) in response to what she saw as women's postwar retreat into the home in a forlorn hope of becoming perfect wives and mothers. American women had been granted the vote in 1919 so that, she regretted, 'for women born after 1920, feminism was dead history'. Not a historian herself, she drew on Eleanor Flexner's *Century of Struggle* (1959), which showed that many early American suffragists had been campaigners for the abolition of slavery and then found that the vote was given (in theory) to emancipated slaves but not to them. The founding moment of their struggle was a women's convention at Seneca Falls, New York State, in 1848, which made historic claims based on a modified version of the Declaration of Independence: 'We hold these truths to be self-evident, that all men *and women* are created equal'. Friedan believed that Flexner's book 'should be required reading for every girl admitted to a US college'.[107]

The student revolts of 1968 did not succeed politically, at least in the short term, but they had a huge impact ideologically and culturally, toppling old gods and opening the way to new thinking on a global scale. From the turmoil arose second-wave feminism, lesbian and gay liberation movements and, in time, transgender liberation movements. Each movement sought to trace its own history in order to draw inspiration from forerunners and to assert legitimacy in the face of those who tried to silence them. These histories were often written by the activists themselves, and some of them entrenched their legitimacy by securing university positions, organizing conferences and publishing journals.

In the United States the Berkshire Conference of Women Historians held a first meeting at Douglass College, Rutgers University, in 1973 and published the proceedings as *Clio's Consciousness Raised* in 1974.[108] One of the organizers, Lois Banner, then published *Women in Modern America: A Brief History*, 'to focus on the dramatic and continuing struggle by determined, innovative women to achieve their rights'.[109] Regularly updated, it was a set text in women's studies departments that proliferated in American universities. Alice Rossi, a feminist and sociologist, published *The Feminist Papers* (1973), an echo of the Founding Fathers' *Federalist Papers*, to lay out the writings of 'a whole host of like-minded women who had preceded my generation in American history', from Abigal Adams to Simone de Beauvoir.[110]

In Britain Sheila Rowbotham, who had been closely involved in the protests of 1968, attended the Tufnell Park Women's Liberation consciousness-raising group from April 1969. Having a history degree from Oxford and teaching for the WEA, she gave a presentation on the role of women in the Paris Commune. She became 'interested in elaborating [her] ideas historically' in order to trace the roots of women's socialism and feminism.[111] At the first Women's Liberation Conference at Ruskin College Oxford she gave a second presentation on women and the 1848 revolution in France. Two years later she published *Women, Resistance and Revolution* as a 'first step towards correcting the masculine bias in the story we have inherited of our revolutionary past'.[112] Jane Rendall, a young lecturer at the University of York who worked on the Scottish Enlightenment, found herself at the Berkshire Conference of Women Historians in the US and decided to teach women's history. She brought out *The Origins of Modern Feminism: Women in Britain, France and the United States*, in 1985.

In France the feminist movement also took off very soon after 1968, but more time passed before women's studies found a foothold in the universities. In the universal Republic where all were equally citizens, the history of women as a separate entity was regarded as a non-subject by the academic establishment. Michelle Perrot, who was a student when *The Second Sex* was published and wanted to research the history of women, was told by her Sorbonne supervisor Ernest Labrousse that this was not possible and so she turned to the labour movement. Fired by the events of 1968, however, and finding a post at the University of Paris VII Jussieu, she co-organized a study group on women's history in 1973, beginning with the question. 'Do women have a history?'.[113] In 1986 she co-signed an essay by a group of women historians in the very establishment journal *Annales* analysing why in France the history of women was still struggling to carve a space for itself.[114] She eventually teamed up with Georges Duby, the leading medieval historian, to co-edit a five-volume *History of Women in the West*. Meanwhile women who had been activists in 1968 and trailblazers of French feminism now began to write the history of women and feminism as the roots of their cause. Annette Lévy-Willard, who became a journalist at the newspaper *Libération*, published a translation of *Living My Life* by the Jewish-American anarchist and feminist Emma Goldman, whom she regarded as a spiritual grandmother.[115] Françoise Picq, who was appointed lecturer at the new university of Paris-Dauphine in 1969, published *Women's Liberation: The Protest Years*, in 1993.[116]

Very soon the feminist movement divided over the question of heterosexuality. While feminists like Sheila Rowbotham and Françoise Picq had close relationships with men, others, like Monique Wittig, argued that heterosexuality was a political regime and that radical feminists must choose lesbianism. Now, they maintained, the history of lesbianism had to be written *against* male sexuality, which was deemed to be based on domination and the denigration of the unmarried woman. Sheila Jeffreys, who was involved in a Women against Violence against Women group in London, explored the period 1880–1930 in *The Spinster and her Enemies* to help 'build a world in which loving women is seen as a positive choice for women, where the spinster and the lesbian are not stigmatised, and in which sexual intercourse and heterosexuality receive no special emphasis as sexual possibilities'.[117]

Also in the slipstream of 1968, a police raid on a gay bar in New York's Greenwich Village triggered four days of the Stonewall Riots as gay activists fought for their rights. The foundation of Gay Liberation Fronts in the US in 1969, in the UK in 1970 and in France as the Homosexual Revolutionary Action Front in 1971 brought in their wake histories of the repression of homosexuals and their campaign for emancipation. Jeffrey Weeks, a member of the Gay Liberation Front in Britain and a researcher at the LSE, published *Coming Out*, a history of homosexual politics in the nineteenth and twentieth centuries, in 1977.[118] French gay activist Jean Le Bitoux later wrote a much more autobiographical history of his own coming out, having been brought up in a repressive bourgeois family, and likening his naval officer father to Admiral Darlan, the Vichy minister who in 1942 brought in a law criminalizing homosexual acts.[119]

In academic circles, the history of women as a social history of their lived experience was eclipsed from the later 1980s by the history of gender. In 1985 Joan Wallach Scott, the founder-director of the Pembroke

Center for Teaching and Research on Women at Brown University, gave an address to the American Historical Association on 'Gender: a useful category of historical analysis'.[120] She provided historical examples for this with her edited collection, *Feminism and History* (1996), in which she argued that 'These identities change over time, vary in different societies, and even change for the same woman depending on the contexts they are in'.[121] Another frontier was opened up in 1990 when American philosopher Judith Butler published *Gender Trouble*. This explained that, living on the East Coast, she 'went to many meetings, bars and marches and saw many kinds of genders, understood myself to be at the crossroads of some of them, and encountered sexuality at several of its cutting edges'.[122]

These interventions gave an academic green light to writing beyond the history of women: the history of feminisms; the history of masculinity; gay, lesbian and transgender history; queer history. It was now understood that feminism could no longer be treated as a bloc but contextualized according to history, geography, class, religion and race. Heidi Safia Mirza, a sociologist from London's South Bank University, criticized 'imperial feminism' and its 'project of domination' and launched studies in Black British Feminism.[123] In 1991 John Tosh and Michael Roper edited *Manful Assertions: Masculinities in Britain Since 1800*. *The Journal of Men's Studies* was launched in 1992 and *Men and Masculinities* journal in 1999. A recurrent theme through the 1990s was 'the crisis of masculinity', generally read historically as a response to women's demands for equality, and given additional traction by psychiatrist Anthony Clare in *On Men: Masculinity in Crisis* (2000). Susan Stryker, a trans woman doing a history PhD at Berkeley, saw it as her goal to dismantle 'a system that relentlessly sorts all of us into biologically based categories deemed more or less worthy of life'. She looked for the history of transgender and from 1991 worked for the Gay and Lesbian History Society in Los Angeles, which in 1999 became the Gay, Lesbian, Bisexual and Transgender History Society, publishing *Transgender History: The Roots of Today's Revolution* in 2017.[124] Fighting the same fight Leslie Finberg, a trans man, published *Transgender Warriors*, which was both a frank history of his own journey and a history of transgender people. His history was to provide legitimation to those who 'defend gender freedom – the right of each individual to express their gender in any way they choose, whether feminine, androgynous, masculine or any point in between'.[125]

This activism and these histories did not go unchallenged. On the contrary. What became known as 'the theory of gender' or 'the ideology of gender' has come in for criticism in conservative circles across the world, where it is portrayed as a threat to the traditional family based on marriage between one man and one woman, and male or female sex determined at birth. Sometimes this has been linked to anti-feminism, such as attempts to limit women's reproductive rights or not protect them from sexual violence. In terms of history-writing, moreover, LGTBQ history or queer history has sometimes set feminist academics against queer academics. In 2021, for example, pressure at the University of Sussex from pro-transgender students led to the resignation of feminist philosophy professor Kathleen Stock: the struggle between feminist history and queer or trans history, caught up as it is in the wider culture wars and was weaponised by those who resist divergence from 'normality' in gender difference.

Black and Indigenous history matters

'Perhaps, in the future, there will be some African history to teach', said Hugh Trevor-Roper, Regius Professor of Modern History at the University of Oxford, in a BBC talk in 1963. 'But at present there is none: there is only the history of the Europeans in Africa. The rest is darkness, like the history of pre-European, pre-Columbian Africa. And darkness is not a subject for history.'[126]

This statement, surprisingly late in time, nevertheless captured a long-dominant view that history was made by white Europeans, who 'discovered' and settled the world, bringing to benighted people Christianity, prosperity and 'civilization'. It stifled the voices of the Indigenous peoples of the Americas and Australasia by dating history from the landing of Columbus in what became the Bahamas in 1492, the landing of the Pilgrim Fathers in Plymouth, Massachusetts, in 1620 and the landing of the First Fleet at Sydney in 1788. Subsequently, Indigenous peoples were driven off their land and often massacred by armed settlers, while slave populations were subjected to brutality and violence.

And yet, from time to time, those subjected peoples did manage to find a voice and tell their story. William Apess, a Pequot Indian, whose tribe in Massachusetts had been deprived of their lands and disintegrated under the influence of rum, himself alternated between 'bad habits', labouring, soldiering and discovering Christianity under the guardianship of a settler family. In 'A Son of the Forest' (1831) he told not only his own story but also that of his people, notably the massacre of the Pequot people by settler militiamen in 1637.[127] Fourteen years later, runaway slave Frederick Douglass published the story of his life. He was separated by a slave-owner from his parents, witnessed his aunt being whipped with 'extraordinary barbarity' by one overseer and saw a slave trying to escape across a river shot by another overseer, so that 'his blood and brains marked the water where he had stood'. Douglass managed to escape to New York in 1830, where he began a new life, read the abolitionist newspaper *The Liberator* and became a propagandist for the anti-slavery movement.[128] The abolition of slavery in 1865 did not end this voicelessness, especially for women. Anna Julia Cooper, born a slave in North Carolina in 1858, went to Oberlin College, Ohio, and taught in Washington's only Black high school. In 1892 she published *A Voice from the South*, in which she remarked that there had been 'no word from the black woman' and arguing that 'the supremacy of one race … cannot ultimately prevail on a continent held in equilibrium by so many and such strong-fibred races as there are struggling on this soil'.[129]

Another element of the Black population were those who migrated to find freedom or to make a better living. Claudia Jones, born in Trinidad in 1915, never wrote a fully-fledged autobiography, but interviews and her journalism survive. Her family emigrated to New York when she was eight, but she grew up in poverty in Harlem and 'early learned on the scourge of indignity stemming from Jim Crow national oppression'. Shocked by the framing of nine Black teenagers from Scottsboro, Alabama, sentenced to death in 1931 for allegedly raping two white girls, she joined the Communist Party, which campaigned against their sentences.[130] She was repeatedly arrested in the McCarthy anti-communist era and finally deported in 1955, sailing to Britain to join the 'Windrush generation' of emigrants from the British Caribbean invited to rebuild Britain after the Second World War. 'I was deported from the USA', she told a London newspaper, 'because as a Negro woman, Communist of West Indian descent, I was a thorn in their side in my opposition to Jim Crow racist discrimination against sixteen million negro Americans in the United States.'[131] In Britain, Jones worked with the Caribbean community, founded the Notting Hill carnival in 1959 as a protest against racist riots, and told West Indians that they needed to find out more about their own history, not that of 'Anglo-Saxon conquests, Sir Walter Raleigh and the feats of royalty' but about 'the Morant Bay anti-slavery rebellion' in Jamaica in 1865.[132]

The voices of Indigenous peoples were also slow to be heard. After removal from their lands and massacres in the United States, Canada and Australia, the children

were from the later nineteenth century separated
from their families and sent to residential schools
in order to assimilate them to the dominant white
race. Charles (Charlie) Perkins, whose mother was
an Aborigine and his absent father Irish and who
described himself as 'one of the original Bastards of
the Bush', was removed from an Aboriginal station
outside Alice Springs at the age of nine or ten in 1945
and sent to a brutal residential school in Adelaide.
'The part-Aboriginal people were nobodies, nothing',
he recalled. 'They took our Aboriginal heritage away
and made us all drifters in society.'[133] He was saved
by football, trialling for Everton in 1959, and by his
studies, getting into the University of Sydney at the
age of twenty-five. He became involved in the Federal
Council for the Advancement of Aborigines and
Torres Strait Islanders (FCAATSI) and was employed
by the Department of Aboriginal Affairs in Canberra,
fighting so hard for Aboriginal civil rights, land rights
and education that he was suspended. He wanted to
build a 'nationhood among the Aboriginal people',
he reflected, 'combining material progress (health,
housing) with cultural balance and identity, with
dignity as the essence'.[134]

In order to be properly heard, Black and Indigenous
voices had to write their own history, defining their
identity and making claims for their legitimacy. Black
history, or Black studies, and later Indigenous studies
needed to become an academic discipline and that
discipline had to challenge white history's centrality
to the curriculum. Carter Godwin Woodson, whose

father had been an enslaved person and who began life as a miner in West Virginia, became the second African American to gain a PhD from Harvard. He published *The Education of the Negro Prior to 1861* (1915) and founded an Association for the Study of Negro Life and History, which brought out the *Journal of Negro History*. 'If you are unable to demonstrate to the world that you have this record', he said in 1921, 'the world will say to you, "You are not worthy to enjoy the blessings of democracy or anything else". They will say to you, "Who are you anyway?"'[135] Woodson taught Black history at segregated Black colleges founded in the Reconstruction era, Howard University in Washington and West Virginia State College. But mainstream history was still defined by historians such as Samuel Eliot Morison of Harvard and Henry Steele Commager of New York University, whose textbook *Growth of the American Republic*, first published in 1930, argued, like Ulrich Bonnell Phillips, that slavery actually civilized African Americans:

> The majority of slaves were apparently happy. There was much to be said for slavery as a transitional status between barbarism and civilization. The negro learned his master's language and accepted in some degree his moral and religious standards. In return he contributed much besides his labour – music and humour for instance – to American civilization.[136]

In the era of the civil rights movement some white historians, often themselves marginalized as Jewish immigrants and communists, contributed by writing scholarly works on slavery and civil rights. Howard Zinn, who was involved in the Student Nonviolent Coordinating Committee (SNCC), was dismissed in 1963 from his professorship at Spelman College, Atlanta, having been accused of radicalizing students, and published *SNCC: The New Abolitionists* the following year. Harvard Sitkoff, who was also involved in the civil rights movement, wrote *A New Deal for Blacks* in 1978. The relay was taken up by African American historians who set Black history in the field African American history, tracing their roots back to African civilizations. Arthur Lee Smith from Georgia, another civil rights activist, who changed his 'slave' name to Molefi Kete Asante after he visited Ghana in 1972, wrote *The Afrocentric Idea* in 1987 and launched a PhD in African American Studies at Temple University, Philadelphia, in 1988.[137] Shortly afterwards, Boston University historians traced the Portuguese and Dutch slave trade back to the Central African kingdoms of Kongo and Ndongo in the sixteenth and seventeenth centuries.[138] Linda Heywood went on to write an acclaimed biography of Njinga, seventeenth-century warrior queen of Ndongo (in present-day Angola), comparing her to Queen Elizabeth I and Catherine the Great and seeing her reign as 'a significant chapter in the history of resistance to colonialism'.[139]

Meanwhile in Britain, Black history and Black studies infiltrated academic life, not directly through history but through cultural studies. Stuart Hall, born in Jamaica, won a Rhodes Scholarship to Oxford in 1951 and was disconcerted when his tutor asked him when he was 'going back'. Later, teaching in a South London secondary school he was shocked, like Claudia Jones, by the race riots of 1958 and became involved in the New Left. As lecturer at the Centre for Contemporary Cultural Studies at the University of Birmingham, he added the lenses of gender and race to that of class. He argued that 'the Caribbean cannot be understood on either side of the Atlantic without taking into account the moment of colonialism and imperialism', although this analysis encountered 'a wall of scepticism and incomprehension from – particularly – scholars of empire', who still argued that the British Empire brought peace, prosperity and civilization.[140] Catherine Hall, married to Stuart in 1964 and initially a feminist historian, headed a research project at University College in 2009–16 on Legacies of British Slave-ownership, which demonstrated how much wealth from the slave plantations had contributed to the hegemony of the British ruling class in the seventeenth and eighteenth centuries.[141]

In Australia it took longer for historians of Aboriginal origin to be appointed to research positions and to write their own history. Marcia Langton, the first Indigenous Australian to graduate with a degree in anthropology, became professor of Aboriginal and Torres Strait Islander Studies at Northern Territory University in 1995. She complained that as a child, history lessons had been a 'terrible burden because ... I learned that people like me were hated, and the only stories told about us provided a steady stock of evidence about our supposedly shockingly violent tendencies, savagery and our innate tendency to steal and pilfer'. She joined forces with film-maker Rachel Perkins, daughter of Charlie Perkins, and they aired *First Australians* as a television series with accompanying book in 2008, giving back to the Aborigines the identity, dignity and history that Charlie had set out to recover thirty years earlier.[142]

The challenge to colonial histories from Black communities and their historians – whether they be Indigenous peoples, immigrants or the descendants of enslaved people – provoked a riposte, if not a backlash, from defenders of white national histories, which had hitherto been dominant. A struggle broke out over the question of national identity and how it was defined by history. Whose history was it anyway? Did it belong to the white people who had run countries and empires or to the Black people who wanted to be part of the national narrative? These struggles were at the forefront of the 'culture wars' and reached a particular intensity from the mid-1990s.

In Australia and Canada debates revolved around the massacre of Indigenous people by settlers and the 'stolen generation' of Indigenous children who were removed from their families to residential schools where violence and sexual abuse were now alleged. Commissions of inquiry reported on the residential schools in Canada in 1996 and Australia in 1997. In Canada it was called a 'national crime'; in Australia it was likened to genocide, a concept much used in the aftermath of genocides in Rwanda (1994) and Bosnia

(1992–95). But in 1996 Liberal prime minister John Howard rejected what he called 'the black armband view of Australian history' and continued, 'I believe the balance sheet of Australian history is a very generous and benign one'. This changed in 2008 when Labour prime minister Kevin Rudd issued a formal apology for the pain inflicted on the Aborigine community in order 'to remove a great stain from the nation's soul and, in a true spirit of reconciliation, to open a new chapter in the history of this great land, Australia'.[143]

In the United States, things were more fraught. The 500th anniversary of Columbus's 'discovery' of the Americas was racked by controversy about whether this was a source of national pride or of national shame. The publication in 1994 of plans by the National History Standards to introduce multiculturalism into school textbooks was denounced by conservatives as the 'bastardization' or 'hijacking' of American history, undermining pride in the American Revolution and democracy. In 2019 *New York Times* journalist Nikole Hannah-Jones launched the 1619 project, persuading the paper to mark the 400th anniversary of the landing of the first slave ship in Jamestown, Virginia, a year before the landing of the *Mayflower*, by putting together a special number, together with podcasts and even a curriculum, that would 'bring slavery and the contributions of Black Americans from the margins of the American story to the centre, where they belong'.[144] This powerful bid to bake slavery into the very founding myth of the American people provoked angry responses from

2.10: Why dates matter

History students do not like learning dates, and Henry Ford described history as 'one damn [or darn] thing after another'. But without chronology, historians could not tell a narrative, which revolves around origins, turning points and endings. Nor could they reliably analyse the causes or consequences of any historical event. Dates, however, may have a political charge which radically changes the narrative or analysis. For some, 1492 stands for Columbus's discovery of the New World; for others, it is the beginning of its colonization and ecological destruction. A history that begins in 1620 foregrounds the Pilgrim Fathers and the foundation of the American colonies, while one that begins in 1619 foregrounds the arrival of the slave ships and the role of slavery in American history. Dates are also divisive. For Protestants, 1688 meant the Glorious Revolution, but for Catholics, another episode in their repression. The same date, 8 May 1945, meant both the end of the Second World War in Europe and the beginning of colonial war in Algeria.

the defenders of that myth. *The Federalist* newspaper launched a rival 1620 project to commemorate the arrival of the *Mayflower* at Plymouth Rock and the Puritan vision of America as 'the shining city upon a hill', acknowledged by Ronald Reagan in his farewell speech of 1989. And Donald Trump created a '1776 Commission' to promote 'patriotic education', warning that 'Failing to identify, challenge, and correct this distorted perspective could fray and ultimately erase the bonds that knit our country and culture together.'[145]

In Britain politicians were keen to congratulate themselves on the 200th anniversary of the abolition of the slave trade in 2007. But a blind eye was turned to the profits gained from slavery, and those campaigning to leave the European Union in 2016 argued that after decades in the doldrums to do so would restore 'global Britain', the 'Anglosphere' of closer relations with the United States and former 'white Dominions' of Canada and Australia, and indeed 'Empire 2.0'. Hostility to immigration and to multicultural Britain provoked the so-called Windrush scandal of 2018, when it was revealed that many people who had migrated legally from the Caribbean in the 1950s and 1960s were now being classified as illegal immigrants and liable to deportation. One of that generation, Jamaican-born poet Linton Kwesi Johnson, who had lived in South London for 55 years, said, 'I'll be crucified for saying this but I believe that racism is very much part of the cultural DNA of this country, and probably has been since imperial times'.[146] The culture war about whether Britain was a monocultural or multicultural country continued.

History written by the victors – so often elite white men – has repeatedly been challenged by groups seeking to define themselves and writing their own history in support of their claims. The streets become a battlefield, but so do schools and universities as champions of new ways of writing history to give a voice to other groups find themselves pitted against defenders of the old ways. Additional conflicts are caused by intersectionality between class, race and gender. Victory may be snatched by a challenging group or school, only to be wrested by another challenger or taken back by the guardian of the citadel. The claim is made that 'you can't rewrite history', but who gets to rewrite history is what is at stake.

3
WHERE DO WE GO FROM HERE?

Working through

History is a battlefield. A battlefield of competing narratives striving to be heard and to come out as Top Story. Historians, like all academics, are engaged in rivalry to ensure that their interpretation of a historical subject gains the most traction. History is also written by non-professional historians and journalists who turn their skills to history writing. The term 'e-history' has been coined to describe the huge number of history podcasts, websites and videos on social media for the consumption of a vast public.[1] The Web is a tremendous vehicle for history stories, but has also been infiltrated by fake history, conspiracy theory and disinformation. The prospect that history essays, articles and even books may in future be written by, or with the help of, Artificial Intelligence tools such as ChatGPT takes these challenges to a new level.

If history were only stories, however, not much would be at stake. History, of course, is based on evidence from the past, and so while the narrative may be constructed, it has to reflect the evidence. Fiction does not require footnotes; history does. History has to be firmly grounded in reliable sources, only a fraction of which have been digitised, and it may be that this is the ultimate weapon against AI. History purports to be truthful; in the words of Ranke, 'what actually happened'. But it is not just that. Ranke modestly said that his task was not to judge the past nor to educate future generations, but it was, and he did.[2] The task of history is to understand, interpret and evaluate the past. This means not just accepting what happened as inevitable and even right, an approach liable to comfort the existing order and its dominant narratives. It means working through the past, in particular its most destructive and divisive episodes, and seeking to learn from them. These episodes include the Holocaust, genocide, colonialism and the climate emergency.

After centuries of chronicling the glories of the three German Reichs, and often with some reluctance, German historians had to come to terms with the fact that their militarism, imperialism and anti-Semitism led to the Holocaust. They even invented a word for it, *Vergangenheitsbewältigung*. West Germany agreed reparations in 1952 to the state of Israel that arose from the ashes of the Holocaust, and a Memorial to the Murdered Jews of Europe was opened in Berlin in 2005. The historians of other countries that had been occupied by or collaborated with Germany during the Second World War also had to recognise their role in the destruction of Europe's Jews. 'Holocaust recognition is our contemporary European entry ticket', said British-American historian Tony Judt, referencing apologies by Poland and Romania ahead of their joining the European Union in 2004 and 2007, respectively.[3] In 2005, in the same spirit, the United Nations General Assembly established International Holocaust Remembrance Day every 27 January.

This 'working through' is far from complete. An anti-Semitism that was supposed to have been erased by knowledge of its consequences was not eliminated; indeed, the myth of the Jewish world conspiracy that can be traced to the fake Protocols of the Elders of Zion still has influence. There has been a rise of far-right movements across Europe which are anti-Semitic and racist. The Muslim terrorists who killed journalists of the French satirical magazine *Charlie Hebdo* in 2015 also killed hostages in a Jewish supermarket. French Jews began to think again about emigrating. Meanwhile there has been a good deal of criticism of the state of Israel for its occupation of Palestinian land. One Israeli historian, now in exile, criticized 'the ethnic cleansing of Palestine'.[4] Those who criticize the state of Israel have nevertheless been accused of anti-Semitism and in 2020 the UK Labour Party was subjected to an Equality and Human Rights Commission inquiry into allegations of anti-Semitism.

Another field where working through is still ongoing is that of sexuality and gender. Women demanded their rights on the grounds of equality; gays and lesbians as an extension of that equality. Gay activist Jean Le Bitoux published a memoir by a homosexual deported by the Nazis because of his sexuality and suggested that homosexuals should therefore be considered, along with Jews and gypsies, as victims of the Holocaust.[5] Feminism, gay rights and trans rights claimed separate identities and those identities, as we have seen, required their own histories. The #MeToo movement changed the game by drawing a new weapon against patriarchy by naming and exposing toxic masculinity and violence against women. Some feminists have been reluctant to acknowledge trans rights, arguing that gender is a matter of biology, and this distinction has been weaponized by the political right, as evidenced by the UK government's blocking of the Scottish Gender Recognition Reform Bill in 2023. The future of this debate will depend on how far the transgender community is able to represent its claims in terms of equal rights, identity or as victims of persecution. To help future research, Gale has published a Women's Studies Archive,[6] a Lesbian Herstory Archive[7] and, more recently, archives of Sexuality and Gender: LGBTQ History and Culture since 1940.[8]

As well as the extermination of the European Jews and the gender war, there is also the pressing issue of slavery and its legacy. Speaking a year after the assault on the Capitol on 6 January 2021 to prevent the democratic passage of power, President Biden appealed to American citizens:

Close your eyes. Go back to that day. What do you see? Rioters rampaging, waving for the first time inside this Capitol a Confederate flag that symbolized the cause to destroy America, to rip us apart. Even during the Civil War that never, ever happened. But it happened here in 2021. This is about making sure the past isn't buried. That's the only way forward. That's what great nations do. They don't bury the past, they face up to it.[9]

The American past he alluded to was its history of slavery, for many its original sin. For some on the right, however, the American Civil War that was fought over slavery was not over, and the Great Replacement Theory warned of the threat of African Americans outnumbering white America. On 17 June 2015 a young white supremacist, Dylann Roof, entered a church in Charleston, South Carolina, and murdered nine Black worshippers. Photographs showed him brandishing the Confederate flag and burning the Union flag. A powerful historical disavowal of this attitude came two months later when Ty Seidule, professor and head of history at West Point military academy, in military uniform and medals, made a five-minute video in which he faced down those who argued that the Civil War was fought not over slavery but over states' rights. 'The evidence is clear and overwhelming', he said. 'Slavery was by a wide margin the most important cause of the Civil War for both sides', and the Secession had been to protect the 'peculiar institution' of slavery. He conceded that slavery was 'the great shame of American history', but urged Americans to confront it.[10] Given that 35 million people viewed this clip, it may be hoped that Americans would indeed take up this challenge.[11] Since then, the 1619 Project, launched by *The New York Times*, has made a powerful case for the landing of the first slaves to be considered the founding moment of the United States although, as we have seen, the push-back from those seeking to defend the traditional founding myth has been powerful.[12]

Figure 3.1: Black Lives Matter rally, H Street, Washington, DC, 4 June 2020, photographed by Tracy Meehleib

The death of George Floyd in Minneapolis on 25 May 2020 triggered worldwide protests against racism, which fed into challenging and reassessing histories of slavery and colonialism.

Slavery was a stain not only on American history but on British history too. In 2012 Barbadian historian Hilary Beckles published a book on *Britain's Black Debt* in respect of slavery and 'native genocide'. He became chair of the Caribbean Community (CARICOM) Reparations Commission to press British and other European governments to recognize their responsibility for 'the victims of slavery and their descendants'.[13] Far from acknowledging this responsibility, the British government turned on the 'Windrush generation' of Caribbeans who had migrated as British subjects to work in Britain, deeming them to be 'illegal immigrants' and deporting many of them to the Caribbean. Further, a 2018 report by Wendy Williams, HM Inspector of Constabulary and Fire and Rescue Services, on mitigating the damage done by the Home Office's 'hostile environment' to immigrants saw most of its recommendations shelved.[14] What was not accomplished by governments has nevertheless been taken up by citizens. Journalists Laura Trevelyan and Alex Renton, together with the descendants of John Gladstone, father of William Gladstone, discovering the names of their ancestors on University College London's database of slave-owners, have made personal reparations to CARICOM.[15]

A fourth (related) major field which has to be worked through is colonialism. In the decade from about 2000, formerly colonized countries successfully argued that they had been the victims of genocide, and postcolonial historians came on board by analysing the occupation, plunder and violence of colonial powers. After 2011, however, there was a riposte by apologists of the Great Replacement Theory, who claimed that Europe and North America were being submerged by migrants of colour and that white civilization was under threat.[16] 'Over the past twenty years,' wrote journalist Kenan Malik in 2023, 'we have witnessed a series of mass murders committed in the name of white nationalism, all primed by conspiracy theories about immigration, Muslims, Jews, the Great Replacement and white genocide.' Malik's response to this was very bold. Race, he argued, is itself a nineteenth-century construct to combat an earlier scare over the perceived threat to the dominant white population of North America and Europe, and identity politics permitted racists to divide 'poor whites' or the 'white working class' from Black people suffering the same inequalities by inviting them to join the white supremacy project. 'Identity politics', he concluded, obscures the 'social and political roots of both working-class inequalities and racial injustices', and campaigners around class and race should now join forces.

This campaign would have no difficulty accessing its own history. Although the iconic member of the working class has been a white man, the working class was, of course, always made up of men and women, white and Black. Women were often at the forefront of the labour struggle, with the strike of the matchgirls at the Bryant & May factory in Bow, East London, in 1888, the strike of *midinettes*, or seamstresses, in Paris in 1917 and the strike of women workers at Fords of Dagenham in 1968. Moreover, women of

Asian origin led the two-year strike at the Grunwick Film Processing Laboratories in West London in 1976–78. In France in 2018 a new version of working-class protest took off with the so-called *gilets jaunes* movement. These were people from small-town and rural France, priced out of the metropolitan cities, ground down by the gig economy, high taxes and the collapse of public services, many hitherto involved with trade unions but now turning to the repertoire of French Revolution, as so many rebels before them.[17] Between January and March 2023, moreover, there was a more traditional labour movement against the government's plans to raise the retirement age from 62 to 64. This was seen to be especially tough on people who joined the workforce straight from school and had physically demanding jobs. Electricity generation stations, oil refineries and petrol depots were shut down, the trains and metro stopped, schools were closed and the binmen walked out, leaving rising piles of rubbish. In Britain, throughout 2022 and 2023, there was a revival of strike action involving railway workers, bus drivers, civil servants, teachers and lecturers, doctors, nurses, ambulance drivers and Amazon workers. Significantly, women overtook men in the membership of trade unions, making up 57 per cent of members in 2020. These changes have been reflected in a revival of historical interest in strike action, the labour movement, the working class and working-class communities.[18]

The new frontier to watch, however, is that of environmental activism and environmental history.

Environmental activists have a long and diverse past, from rural campaigns to defend forests in India from 1910, Greenpeace interference with French nuclear testing in the Pacific in the 1980s and protest of Cree Indians against a Canadian hydroelectric scheme in 1990. However, a new chapter in response to the twenty-first century climate emergency was opened in 2018 with the launch of Extinction Rebellion (XR) in Britain, soon spreading to other parts of Europe, North America, Latin America, Africa, Japan and Australia.

Activists have written their own histories of how they became involved and their role in the movement. Greta Thunberg was only 15 when she addressed an XR rally in London in 2018:

When I was about eight years old I first heard about something called climate change or global warming. ... No one ever talked about it, ever. To me it did not add up. It was too unreal. I have Asperger's syndrome and to me, almost everything is in black and white. I think in many ways autistic people are the normal ones and the rest of the people are pretty strange. They keep saying that climate change is an existential threat and the most important issue of all. And yet they just carry on like before. ... Everything needs to change. And it has to start today. So everyone out there: it is now time for civil disobedience. It is time to rebel.[19]

Because environmental protest has such a long pedigree, so does environmental history. But it is a diverse history. A benign view was nostalgia for the unspoiled landscape that was then ruined by American 'civilization'. Roderick Nash's *Wilderness and the American Mind* (1967) warned that the planet was becoming a wasteland and dreamed of a world that is 'once again almost wild'.[20] A tougher view, taken by Alfred Crosby in *The Columbian Exchange* and William Cronon in *Changes in the Land*, argued that the European invasion of the Americas decimated the Indigenous Indian populations by imported diseases, drove them off their land, turned their resources into commodities, and degraded their time-honoured ecology.[21] Research brought together scholars from the West and those from the developing world. Thus Ramachandra Guha, who had written his PhD on the Chipko movement of women in Utterakhand defending their forests bordering the Himalayas from industrial logging in the 1970s, joined with David Arnold to edit *Nature, Culture, Imperialism*.[22] A similar alliance is taking place in campaigning too, with XR activists from the West joining forces with Indigenous peoples in order to secure the future of all humanity on the planet. This history has yet to be written. The XR activists may be portrayed as the new Chartists, the new suffragettes, the new civil rights protesters. They may combine the anti-colonialist and environmental narrative in a new history that will surpass the Marxist narrative of proletarian revolution as the dominant story of the twenty-first century. The flame passes to a new generation of historians.

Who writes history?

Historians have their work cut out. As we have seen, they are busy myth-busting, wrestling with the duty to write objective history and the reality that all history writing is political, navigating the sensitive and also politically charged pathways of history and identity. But they are not alone.

True, some of them may live in ivory towers, but these are connected to social media and the World Wide Web, a changing landscape of e-history which offers huge possibilities but also huge challenges. Possibilities, because historians now have the option of making content for history podcasts, of which 240 were already counted in 2020.[23] Challenging, because there are hundreds of thousands of stories out there, some true but many false, spreading lies, conspiracy theories and disinformation. Some are helpful, such as Ty Seidule's 2015 account of the American Civil War; others are dangerous, such as sites or chats that deny the Holocaust, argue that vaccines are dangerous or that America is controlled by a cabal of paedophiles, or promote the agendas of populist leaders worldwide. Equally dangerous are regimes that shut down historical research and debate, whether in China, with its denunciation of 'historical nihilism', or in the UK, with warnings that 'you can't rewrite history'.

Professional historians do not stand still but are constantly rewriting history in the light of new questions, new evidence and new methods. They are, as we have seen, engaged with ongoing conversations and debates with other historians as to the most accurate and persuasive interpretation. Historians work in institutions in which curriculum reform takes place periodically, and often controversially, as history teaching seeks to realign itself with new perspectives and methods that emerge from developments in society relating to power and identity. Social, economic and labour history came onto history syllabuses in the 1960s and 1970s, women's history arrived in the 1970s and 1980s, gender history and queer history in the 1990s, global history, postcolonial history and Black history after 2000. There are ongoing discussions about decolonizing the curriculum and queering the curriculum which will continue into the future, not without push-back from those defending white, straight history.[24]

In schools there have also been curriculum developments. There is a rigidity about the national curriculum and pressure from government to teach the history of empire in a 'balanced' way. But it is now possible, for example, to study an AQA GCSE history option on 'Migration, empires and the people, c. 790 to the present' alongside more traditional options such as 'America 1840–1895: expansion and consolidation'. Highly original also was a 2014 'History Lessons' project pioneered by Professors Claire Alexander and Joya Chatterji. 'Who and what are included in "British history" and who or what are excluded? How does "our island story" engage with centuries of migration to and from its shores?', they asked. 'Our island story is necessarily a globalised one, and has always been, and Britain itself has always been, ethnically, culturally and socially diverse.'[25] The project targeted British cities with large immigrant populations, including London, Manchester, Sheffield, Leicester and Cardiff, and took school children on guided walks and visits to explore the history of their neighbourhood with the help of teachers, museum staff and film-makers. They discovered how their history and the history of their families and communities were shaped by global trade, industry, slavery, empire and migration. Rather than feeling excluded by the history of the Tudors and Stuarts, one teacher said, children whose families came from overseas 'can see themselves reflected back in the history classroom'.[26]

This project highlights an important interface between academic history, schools and history in the community. The study of community history, family history and individual history trains people in historical methods such as collecting and weighing evidence, historical analysis and exposition. It 'takes back control' of history-writing from the powers that have traditionally done this for us and pushes beyond some of the simplicities of identity history to demonstrate the diversity of communities and complexities of heritage that are not simply working class or middle class, white or Black, gay or straight.

A powerful example of community history was *Ask the Fellows Who Cut the Hay* (1956), an oral history of Blaxhall, a Suffolk farming village, by George Ewart Evans, who arrived there from South Wales when his wife was appointed a teacher. Motivated by nostalgia for a rural way of life, it responded to an early oral history concern for 'the world we have lost'.[27] Local and community histories have been sustained by the Historical Association, founded in 1906, and the Oral History Society, founded in 1973, with early oral history groups set up in Ambleside in 1976 and Waltham Forest in 1983. Community histories were also undertaken by the external studies arms of universities, discovering, like Alexander and Chatterji, the global in the local. In 2017, for example, Priya Atwal of the University of Oxford undertook a project on the Indian Army in the First World War through the lens of the Oxfordshire and Buckinghamshire Light Infantry, working with the Soldiers of Oxfordshire Museum, the Oxford University Sikh Society, the Oxford Muslim Community Initiative and the Oxford Hindu Temple Project.[28]

Family history, the discovery of our ancestry, provides a powerful explanation of who we are. Genealogy has a long and distinguished pedigree, but the art for the historian is to link to wider historical contexts such as slavery, colonialism, world wars, migration and genocide. Alex Haley's *Roots*, published in 1976, told the semi-fictionalized story of his ancestor, Kunta Kinte, who was captured in The Gambia, sold into slavery and transported to the American plantations. It topped the best-seller list, was made into a television series and stimulated research into African American history.[29] Stuart Hall, born into a middle-class family in Jamaica, felt like 'the last colonial'. He did not think of himself as Black until he went to England, confronted by the racism of a declining imperial nation which he felt intensely when he met Catherine on a Campaign for Nuclear Disarmament (CND) march. His twin goals were to 'change British society' in a multicultural direction and 'found a new family'.[30]

Two complementary accounts of discovering Jewish roots have been offered by international lawyer Philippe Sands and writer Katja Petrowskaja. Sands' grandfather, born in Lemberg (now Lviv, Ukraine) in 1904, was expelled from Vienna after the Anschluss, fled to Paris and fought in the French foreign legion and French resistance, while his grandmother went into hiding and his mother Ruth, born in 1938, was hidden by an Englishwoman. Sands was particularly interested in the crossover of his grandfather's life with that of Rafael Lemkin, also from Lemberg and Vienna, and the theorist of genocide.[31] The task of Katya Petrowskaja is harder, reassembling the story of her family in *Maybe Esther* from the 'rubble of history' that remained after the Holocaust in Poland, Ukraine and Russia. A young woman living in Berlin, she returned to Warsaw, where her great-grandmother, 'maybe' called Esther, and too infirm to escape, was 'maybe' shot by Germans in the city streets. She also went to Kyiv, from where her grandmother Rosa fled with her own mother in 1941, and to Moscow, where her great-uncle shot dead a German diplomat in 1932, and she discovered that fight and flight often intersected in the family history of European Jews.[32]

Individual memoirs are the account of one person's life, but they are never freestanding. They often begin with the family history that has shaped them and then place their developing lives in historical contexts. The lives of activists we encountered in Chapter 2 from William Lovett to Frederick Douglass and Leslie Finberg, do exactly that. Individual memoirs may explore with some sensitivity the intersection of class, gender and race. Vera Brittain, whose brother and fiancé were both killed in the First World War, explored the impact of the war on her generation of young men and women in her *Testament of Youth* (1933).[33] Fifty years later Carolyn Steedman disrupted the genre of the working-class memoir by juxtaposing the childhood of her own mother, a Lancashire weaver's daughter who came to London in 1934 for a better life, and her own, escaping her drab life in Streatham to go to university in the 1960s.[34]

Of course, not everyone is able to write a memoir of such subtlety and scale about a generation. The field of public history, however, holds that anyone and everyone can write a life story or fragment of it from the bits and pieces that people collect. Hilda Kean began her research when she was clearing out her mother's house after she went into a nursing home, and discovered letters, photographs, diaries, school reports, ornaments, souvenirs and other possessions. From that she was able to tell a life story of a working-class woman from Epping Forest and of the world in which she lived.[35] The story did not have to support or refute a 'grand narrative' such as *The Making of the English Working Class*; the meaning was whatever could be constructed from the bric-à-brac. Above all, public history is based on the idea that all people are active agents in the creation of history. Leopold von Ranke said that one of the tasks of historians was 'instructing the present for the benefit of future ages'. But present and future ages also have to instruct themselves. Whether as reader or writer, podcaster or contributor to social media, 'everyone is a historian'.[36]

NOTES

Chapter 1

1   Vladimir Putin, 'On the Historical Unity of Russians and Ukrainians', 12 July 2021, http://en.kremlin.ru/events/president/news/66181 (accessed 09/11/2022).

2   Vladimir Putin, 'On the Historical Unity of Russians and Ukrainians'.

3   Vladmir Putin, Address, 21 Feb. 2021, http://en.kremlin.ru/events/president/news/67828 (accessed 15/2/2023).

4   Joe Biden, Remarks by President Biden on the United Effort of the Free World to support the People of Ukraine, 26 Mar. 2022, https://www.whitehouse.gov/briefing-room/speeches-remarks/2022/03/26/remarks-by-president-biden-on-the-united-efforts-of-the-free-world-to-support-the-people-of-ukraine/ (accessed 15/02/2023).

5   Shaun Walker, *The Long Hangover: Putin's New Russia and the Ghosts of the Past* (Oxford: OUP, 2018), 10, 245.

6   Timothy Snyder, *The Road to Unfreedom: Russia, Europe, America* (London: Vintage, 2018).

7   See for example, Rhoddri Jeffreys-Jones, *The CIA and American Democracy* (1989, 2003); Vincent Bevins, *The Jakarta Method: Washington's Anticommunist Crusade and the Mass Murder Program that Shaped Our World* (New York: PublicAffairs, 2020) and Susan Williams, *White Malice: The CIA and the Neocolonisation of Africa* (London: Hurst & Co, 2021).

8   Mark Edele, 'Fighting Russia's History Wars: Vladimir Putin and the Codification of World War II', *History and Memory* 29(2) (Fall/Winter 2017), 90–124.

9   Mikhail Sokolov and Robert Coalson, '"A Dangerous Commission": Russian Historians Alarmed as Putin Creates State Body on 'Historical Education', Radio Free Europe/Radio Liberty, 10 Aug. 2021 https://www.rferl.org/a/russia-history-commission-putin/31403236.html (accessed 10/11/2022).

10 Glenn Tiffert, 'Thirty Years after Tiananmen: Memory in the Era of Xi Jinping', *Journal of Democracy* 30(2) (April 2019), 38–49 https://www.journalofdemocracy.org/articles/30-years-after-tiananmen-memory-in-the-era-of-xi-jinping/ (accessed 10/11/2022).

11 Klaus Mühlhahn, *Making China Modern. From the Great Qing to Xi Jinping* (Cambridge, MA: Belknap Press of Harvard UP, 2019), 516–21; Peter Frankopan, *The Silk Roads. A New History of the World* (London: Bloomsbury, 2015), 516–21; Frankopan, *The New Silk Roads. The Present and Future of the World* (London: Bloomsbury, 2018).

12 Robert Gildea, *Empires of the Mind. The Colonial Past and the Politics of the Present* (Cambridge: CUP, 2019), 219.

13 David Cannadine, 'The Context, Performance and Meaning of Ritual: The British Monarchy and the Invention of Tradition, c. 1820–1977', in Eric Hobsbawm and Terence Ranger (eds), *The Invention of Tradition* (Cambridge: CUP, 1983), 101–64, 124.

14 George Orwell, *Nineteen Eighty-Four* (London: Secker & Warburg, 1949), ch 3.

15 https://www.independent.co.uk/news/uk/politics/boris-johnson-bbc-proms-rule-britannia-lyrics-row-british-history-black-lives-matter-a9687816.html (accessed 20/11/2020).

16 Catherine Hall, Nicholas Draper, Keith McClelland, Katie Donington and Rachel Lang, *Legacies of British Slave-Ownership. Colonial Slavery and the Formation of Victorian Britain* (Cambridge: CUP, 2014), 2–37.

17 David Olusoga, *Black and British. A Forgotten History* (London: Macmillan, 2016), xv–xix, 517–19.

18 Nigel Biggar, *Colonialism. A Moral Reckoning* (London: William Collins, 2023), 53–66, 297, 289.

19 Juana Summers, National Public Radio, 24 Nov. 2020, https://www.npr.org/2020/11/24/938187233/trump-push-to-invalidate-votes-in-heavily-black-cities-alarms-civil-rights-group (accessed 30/11/2020).

20 *Washington Post*, 26 Oct. 2021.

Chapter 2

1 Margaret MacMillan, *The Uses and Abuses of History* (London: Profile Books, 2009), 81.

2 Ernest Renan, 'Qu'est-ce Qu'une nation?' in John Hutchinson and Anthony D. Smith, *Nationalism* (Oxford and New York: Oxford University Press, 1994), 17.

3   Frederick Merk, *Manifest Destiny and Mission in American History. A Reinterpretation* (New York: Vintage Books, 1963), 32.

4   W.E.B. Du Bois, 'The Souls of the White Folk', in *Darkwater. Voices from within the Veil* (London and New York: Verso, 2016), 17–29.

5   Richard Storry, *A History of Modern Japan* (London: Penguin, 1960), 23.

6   Tacitus, *Agricola and Germany* (Oxford: Oxford University Press, 1999), 38, 62.

7   Georg Lukács, *The Historical Novel* (London: Merlin Press, 1962), 19–26; Walter Scott, *Ivanhoe* (Oxford: Oxford University Press, 1996), 26.

8   *Geschichte der romanischen und germanischen Völker von 1494 bis 1535* (Leipzig und Berlin, 1824), v–vi. I am grateful to George Miller for offering this translation.

9   John Kenyon, *The History Men. The Historical Profession in England since the Renaissance* (London: Weidenfeld & Nicolson, 1993), 149–55, 170–4.

10 Sharon Turner, *The History of the Anglo-Saxons from the Earliest Period to the Norman Conquest* (7th edition, London: Longman, 1852), III, 160.

11 Hubert Howe Bancroft, *History of California* (7 vols, San Francisco: A.L. Bancroft, 1884–90).

12 Julian Hawthorne, *The History of the United States from 1492 to 1910. Vol I. From the Discovery of America to the Battle of Lexington* (New York and London: The Cooperative Publication Society, 1898), 5.

13 Charles-Victor Langlois and Charles Seignobos, *Introduction to the Study of History* (New York: Henry Holt, 1932), 17.

14 Arthur Bryant, *English Saga, 1840–1940* (London: The Reprint Society, 1942), 339; A.L. Rowse, *The Spirit of English History* (London: Jonathan Cape, 1943).

15 Herbert Butterfield, *Man on his Past. The Study of the History of Historical Scholarship* (CUP, 1955), 30.

16 Boyd C. Schafer, *Nationalism. Myth and Reality* (London: Victor Gollancz, 1955), 7.

17 Eric Hobsbawm and Terence Ranger (eds), *The Invention of Tradition* (CUP, 1983), 1–13.

18 David Reynolds, *In Command of History. Churchill Fighting and Writing the Second World War* (London: Allen Lane, 2004), 169.

19 Frantz Fanon, *The Wretched of the Earth* (Harmondsworth: Penguin, 1990).

20   Edward Saïd, *Orientalism. Western Conceptions of the Orient* (London: Penguin, 1995).

21   Gayatri Chakravorty Spivak, 'Can the Subaltern Speak?' in Cary Nelson and Lawrence Grossberg (eds), *Marxism and the Interpretation of Culture* (Urbana: University of Illinois Press, 1988), 271–313.

22   Bernard Lewis, 'The Roots of Muslim Rage', *The Atlantic*, Sept. 1990.

23   Samuel P. Huntington, 'The Clash of Civilizations?', *Foreign Affairs*, 72(3) (Summer, 1993); Huntington, *The Clash of Civilizations and the Remaking of World Order* (New York, Simon & Schuster, 1996).

24   Niall Ferguson, *Empire. How Britain Made the Modern World* (London: Allen Lane, 2003), 370.

25   Ferguson, *Colossus: The Rise and Fall of the American Empire* (London: Penguin, 2005), viii–x.

26   Caroline Elkins, *Britain's Gulag. The Brutal End of the Empire in Kenya* (London: Pimlico, 2005); David Anderson, *Histories of the Hanged. Britain's Dirty War in Kenya and the End of Empire* (London: Phoenix, 2006). See also Ian Cobain, *Cruel Britannia: A Secret History of Torture* (London: Portobello, 2012).

27   Andrew Roberts, *A History of the English-Speaking Peoples since 1900* (London: Weidenfeld & Nicolson, 2006).

28   Jean Raspail, 'Big Other', preface to *Le Camp des Saints* (Paris, Laffont, 2011), 25–38.

29   http://www.liberation.fr/france/2015/09/16/le-livre-de-chevet-de-marine-le-pen-decrit-une-apocalypse-migratoire_1383026; https://www.huffingtonpost.co.uk/entry/steve-bannon-camp-of-the-saints-immigration_us_58b75206e4b0284854b3dc03

30   Jean Camus, *Le Grand Remplacement* (Neuilly-sur-Seine, D. Reinharc, 2011).

31   Bruce Gilley, 'The Case for Colonialism', *Academic Questions*, 31 (2018), 167–85.

32   Shashi Tharoor, *Inglorious Empire: What the British did to India* (London: Hurst & Co., 2017); Priyamvada Gopal, *Insurgent Empire: Anticolonial Resistance and British Dissent* (London and New York: Verso, 2019); Priya Satia, *Time's Monster: History, Conscience and Britain's Empire* (London: Allen Lane, 2020), 138; George Bernard Shaw, 'The Man of Destiny' in *Plays Pleasant* (London: Penguin, 1946), 205–6.

33 Caroline Elkins, *Legacy of Violence: A History of the British Empire* (London: The Bodley Head, 2022), 16, 127–62.

34 Biggar, *Colonialism* (London: William Collins, 2023), 297.

35 See Chapter 1, n 14.

36 E.H. Carr, *What is History?* (London: Penguin, 1961), 22.

37 Nigel Saul, *Richard II* (New Haven & London: Yale UP, 1997), 376–7.

38 Christopher Hill, 'Sir Edward Coke myth-maker' in Hill, *Intellectual Origins of the English Revolution* (Oxford: Clarendon Press, 1980), 246; J.G.A. Pocock, *The Ancient Constitution and the Feudal Law* (Bath: Cedric Chivers, 1957), 43–5.

39 Christopher Hill, 'The Norman Yoke' in Hill, *Puritanism and Revolution: Studies in the Interpretation of the English Revolution in the 17th Century* (London: Secker and Warburg, 1958), 50–122.

40 John Milton, *Political Writings* (ed. Martin Dzelzainis) (Cambridge: CUP, 1991), 171.

41 Edward Hyde, Lord Clarendon, *The History of the Great Rebellion* (ed. Roger Lockyer) (Oxford: OUP, 1967), 455.

42 Bridget Hill, *The Republican Virago. The Life and Times of Catharine Macaulay, Historian* (Oxford: Clarendon Press, 1992), 35–6.

43 James Madison, Alexander Hamilton and John Jay, *The Federalist Papers* (ed. Isaac Kramnick) (London: Penguin, 1987), 118–21.

44 Saint-Just, 'Discours concernant le jugement de Louis XVI, 13 nov. 1792', in Ch. Vellay, *L'Élite de la Révolution* (Paris: Fasquelle, 1908), 364–72.

45 Robespierre, Speech to the Convention, 5 Feb. 1794, in *Discours et Rapports à la Convention* (Paris: Union Générale des Éditions, 1965), 214.

46 Edmund Burke, *Reflections on the Revolution in France* (London: Pelican Books, 1968), 117.

47 Tom Paine, *The Rights of Man* (London: Penguin, 1969), 64, 87–8.

48 Lord Macaulay, *The History of England* (London: Penguin, 1986), 295.

49 Karl Marx, 'Towards a Critique of Hegel's Philosophy of Right: Introduction' (David McClellan, ed.), *Karl Marx Early Texts* (Oxford: Blackwell, 1972), 117.

50 Karl Marx and Friedrich Engels, 'The Manifesto of the Communist Party', in Marx and Engels, *Selected Works in One Volume* (London: Lawrence & Wishart, 1968), 35, 46.

51 Jefferson Davis, *The Essential Writings* (ed. William J. Cooper) (New York: The Modern Library, 2003).

52 Abraham Lincoln, Gettysburg Address, 19 Nov. 1863, in Lincoln, *Complete Works X* (ed by John G. Nicolay and John Hay) (1905), 209–10.

53 Charles and Mary Beard, *The Rise of American Civilization* (London: Jonathan Cape, 1977), II, 53–4.

54 Ulrich Bonnell Phillips, *Life and Labor of the Old South* (Boston: Little, Brown and Co., 1929), 195–9.

55 Claude G. Bowers, *The Tragic Era: The Revolution after Lincoln* (New York: Blue Ribbon Books, 1929), vi.

56 J.G. Randall, *The Civil War and Reconstruction* (Boston: D.C. Heath and Co., 1937), 690, 847.

57 Martin Luther King, 'I Have a Dream', Washington, DC, 28 Aug. 1963, in Brian MacArthur (ed.), *Great Speeches of the Twentieth Century* (London: Penguin, 2012), 328–33.

58 Kenneth M. Stampp, *The Peculiar Institution: Negro Slavery in the American South* (London: Eyre and Spottiswoode, 1964), 397.

59 Stampp, *The Era of Reconstruction. America after the Civil War, 1865–77* (London: Eyre and Spottiswoode, 1965), 184–5.

60 Gary W. Gallagher, *The Confederate War* (Cambridge, MA, Harvard UP, 1997); Karen L. Cox, *Dreaming of Dixie. How the South was Created in American Popular Culture* (U.N. Carolina Press, 2011).

61 Karl Marx, 'The Eighteenth Brumaire of Louis Bonaparte', in Marx and Engels, *Selected Works in One Volume*, 170.

62 Karl Marx, 'The Civil War in France' (1871) in Marx and Engels, *Selected Works in One Volume*, 307.

63 V.I. Lenin, *What is to be Done?* (London: Penguin, 1988), 143–7.

64 Jay Bergman, *The French Revolutionary Tradition in Russian and Soviet Politics, Political Thought and Culture* (Oxford: OUP, 2019), 90.

65 Lenin, 'The State and Revolution' in Lenin, *Selected Works* (Moscow: Progress Publishing, 1968), 286–93.

66 John Reed, *Ten Days that Shook the World* (London: Communist Party of Great Britain, 1926), introduction.

67 William Chamberlin, *The Russian Revolution* [1935] (2 vols, New York: Macmillan, 1957), 121; Chamberlain, *The Soviet Union* (London: Duckworth, 1930), 424–5.

68 Chamberlin, *Confessions of an Individualist* (London: Duckworth, 1940), 151–2, 170.

69 Leon Trotsky, *The Revolution Betrayed* (London: New Park Publications, 1973), 105, 278.

70 Simon Sebag Montefiore, *Stalin. The Court of the Red Tsar* (London: Weidenfeld & Nicolson, 2003), 483.

71 Robert Conquest, *The Great Terror: Stalin's Purge of the Thirties* (London: Macmillan, 1968), xiii.

72 Roy Medvedev, *Let History Judge: The Origins and Consequences of Stalinism* (Oxford: Oxford UP, 1989), 585–7.

73 Christopher Hill, *The English Revolution 1640. An Essay* (London: Lawrence and Wishart, 1955), 6.

74 Blair Worden, 'The Puritan Revolution' in Worden (ed.), *Hugh Trevor-Roper: The Historian* (London and New York: I.B. Tauris, 2016).

75 C.V. Wedgwood, *The Trial of Charles I* (London: Folio Society, 1959), 24.

76 M.J. Gorbachev, 'Report to the 27th Congress of the CSPU', in Gorbachev, *Speeches and Writings* (Oxford: Pergamon Press, 1986), 3–96.

77 Reynald Sécher, *Le Génocide franco-français: La Vendée-Vengé* (Paris: PUF, 1986).

78 Robert Gildea, *The Past in French History* (New Haven and London: Yale University Press, 1994), 15.

79 Robert Service, *Kremlin Winter: Russia and the Second Coming of Vladimir Putin* (London: Picador, 2019), 27.

80 Mao Zedong, 'On the Work-Study programme in Hunan', in Stuart Schram (ed.), *Mao's Road to Power. Revolutionary Writings 1912–1949. Vol. I, The Pre-Marxist Period 1912–20* (New York: Armonk and London: M.E. Sharpe, 1992), 454.

81 Mao Zedong, 'Some Points for Attention in Commemorating the Paris Commune', 18 Mar. 1926, in Stuart Schram (ed.), *Mao's Road to Power. Revolutionary Writings. Vol. II, National Revolution and Social Revolution 1920–27* ((New York: Armonk and London: M.E. Sharpe, 1994), 365–8. Most historians agree that there were between 10,000 and 20,000 deaths.

82 Joan Robinson, *The Cultural Revolution in China* (London: Penguin, 1969), 24–5.

83 William Hinton, *Hundred Day War: The Cultural Revolution in Tsinghua University* (New York and London: Monthly Review Press, 1972), 7.

84 Stuart Schram, *Mao Tse-tung Unrehearsed. Talks and Letters, 1956–71* (London: Penguin, 1974), 258.

[85] Deng Xiaoping, Address to officers at the rank of general and above commanding troops enforcing martial law in Beijing, 9 June 1989, https://www.marxists.org/reference/archive/deng-xiaoping/1989/5.htm (accessed 28/02/23).

[86] Claudie and Jacques Broyelle, *China: A Second Look* (Brighton: Harvester Press, 1980), 139.

[87] Anne F. Thurston, *Enemies of the People* (New York: Alfred Kopf, 1987), xv.

[88] Zheng Yi, *Scarlet Memorial. Tales of Cannibalism in Modern China* (Boulder, CO: Westview Press, 1996), xii, 14–15.

[89] Roderick MacFarquhar and Michael Schoenhals, *Mao's Last Revolution* (Cambridge, MA: Belknap Press of Harvard UP, 2006), 131.

[90] *Global Voices*, 29 Mar. 2014.

[91] Email from Professor Patricia Thornton, 14 June 2023.

[92] Pieter Geyl, *Napoleon: For and Against* (London: Jonathan Cape, 1949).

[93] James Kay-Shuttleworth, *The Moral and Physical Condition of the Working Classes employed in the Cotton Manufacture of Manchester* (London: J. Ridgway, 1832), 7.

[94] Friedrich Engels, *The Condition of the Working Class in England* (Oxford: Blackwell, 1958), 149, 258.

[95] Prosper-Olivier Lissagaray, *History of the Commune*, tr. Eleanor Marx-Aveling (London: Reeves and Turner, 1886), 393, 458–9.

[96] Louise Michel, *Mémoires* (Brussels, Éditions du Tribord, 2005), 397.

[97] August Bebel, *My Life* (London: T. Fisher Unwin, 1912), 292.

[98] Samuel Gompers, *Seventy Years of Life and Labour: An Autobiography* (New York: E.P. Dutton, 1925), 61, 154.

[99] Will Thorne, *My Life's Battles* (London: George Newnes, 1925), 72, 87.

[100] Beatrice Webb, *My Apprenticeship* (New York: Longmans, 1926), 390.

[101] E.P. Thompson, *The Making of the English Working Class* (London: Penguin, 1968) 13.

[102] Jane Austen, *Persuasion* [1818] (Oxford, OUP, 1998), 188.

[103] Louise Michel, *Mémoires*, 43, 120

[104] Emmeline Pankhurst, *My Own Story* (London: Eveleigh Nash, 1914), 148, 269.

[105] Simone de Beauvoir, *The Second Sex* (London: Jonathan Cape, 1953), 106.

106 Juliet Mitchell, *Women. The Longest Revolution* (London: Virago, 1984), 53.

107 Eleanor Flexner, *Century of Struggle:. The Women's Rights Movement in the United States* (revised edition, Cambridge, MA and London: Belknap Press of Harvard UP, 1975), 71–7; Betty Friedan, *The Feminine Mystique* [1963] (London: Victor Gollancz, 1971), 100, 380.

108 Mary Hartman and Lois Banner, *Clio's Consciousness Raised: New Perspectives on the History of Women* (New York, Harper Torchbooks, 1974).

109 Lois Banner, *Women in Modern America: A Brief History* (second edition, San Diego: Harcourt Brace Jovanovich, 1984), v.

110 Alice Rossi, *The Feminist Papers: From Adams to De Beauvoir* (New York: Bantam Books, 1973), xi.

111 Sheila Rowbotham, *Promise of a Dream: Remembering the Sixties* (London: Penguin, 2000), 245.

112 Sheila Rowbotham, *Women, Resistance and Revolution* (London: Allen Lane, 1972), 1.

113 Georges Duby and Michelle Perrot, 'Écrire l'histoire des femmes', in Duby and Perrot (eds) *Histoire des femmes en Occident I* (Paris: Plon, 1991), viii–ix.

114 Cécile Dauphin et al, 'Culture et pouvoir des femmes: essai d'historiographie', *Annales* 41 (1986), 271–93.

115 Cathy Bernheim and Annette Lévy-Willard, *Emma Goldman: Épopée d'une anarchiste (New York 1886–Moscou 1920)* (Paris: Hachette, 1979).

116 Françoise Picq, *La Libération des Femmes. Les années-mouvement* (Paris: Seuil, 1993).

117 Sheila Jeffreys, *The Spinster and her Enemies. Feminism and Sexuality, 1880–1930* (London: Pandora, 1985), 196.

118 Jeffrey Weeks, *Coming Out: Homosexual Politics in Britain from the Nineteenth Century to the Present* (London: Quartet Books, 1977).

119 Jean Le Bitoux, *Citoyen de la Seconde Zone: Trente ans de lutte pour la reconnaissance de l'homosexualité en France* (Paris: Hachette, 2003), 13–17.

120 Joan Wallach Scott, 'Gender: A Useful Category of Historical Analysis', *American Historical Review* 91(5) (1986), 1053–75.

121 Joan Wallach Scott (ed.), *Feminism and History* (Oxford and New York: OUP, 1996), 5.

122   Judith Butler, *Gender Trouble: Feminism and the Subversion of Identity* (New York and London: Routledge, 1990), xvi.

123   Heidi Safia Mirza (ed.), *Black British Feminism: A Reader* (London: Routledge, 1997), 5, 9.

124   Susan Stryker, *Transgender History. The Roots of Today's Revolution* (2nd edn, New York: Seal Press, 2017).

125   Leslie Feinberg, *Transgender Warriors* (Boston: Beacon Press, 1996), x, 3–11, 103.

126   Hugh Trevor-Roper, 'The Rise of Christian Europe', *The Listener*, 70/1809, 28 Nov. 1963, 871, republished with small qualifications in *The Rise of Christian Europe* (London, Thames & Hudson, 1965), 9.

127   Barry O'Connell (ed.), *On Our Own Ground. The Complete Writings of William Apess, a Pequot* (Amherst, MA: University of Massachusetts Press, 1992), 4–56.

128   Solomon Northup, *Twelve Years a Slave with the Narrative of the Life of Frederick Douglass, an American slave, written by himself* (Ware, Hertfordshire: Wordsworth Editions, 2015), 242–320.

129   Anna Julia Cooper, *A Voice from the South* (New York: Oxford University Press, 1988), 167.

130   Claudia Jones, 'Autobiographical History', in Carole Boyce Davies (ed.), *Claudia Jones, Beyond Containment. Autobiographical Reflections, Essays and Poems* (Banbury: Ayebia Clarke Publishing, 2011), 10–16.

131   Claudia Jones, interview with *Caribbean News*, June 1956, in *Claudia Jones, Beyond Containment*, 16.

132   Claudia Jones, 'The Caribbean Community in Britain', *Freedomways*, summer 1964, in *Claudia Jones, Beyond Containment*, 180.

133   Charles Perkins, *A Bastard Like Me* (Sydney: Ure Smith, 1975), 14, 31.

134   Perkins, *A Bastard Like Me*, 193; see also Peter Read, *Charles Perkins. A Biography* (Ringwood, Victoria: Viking, 1990).

135   August Meier and Elliott Rudwick, *Black History and the Historical Profession, 1915–1980* (Urbana and Chicago, IL: University of Illinois Press, 1986), 9.

136   Samuel Eliot Morison and Henry Steele Commager, *Growth of the American Republic* (first edition, New York: Oxford University Press, 1930), 413, 418.

137   Molefi Kete Asante, *The Afrocentric Idea* (revised and expanded edition, Philadelphia: Temple University Press, 1998).

138 Linda Heywood and John K. Thornton, *Central Africans, Atlantic Creoles and the Founding of the Americas, 1585–1660* (Cambridge: CUP, 2007).

139 Linda Heywood, *Nzinga of Angola. Africa's Warrior Queen* (Cambridge, MA: Harvard UP, 2017), 3.

140 Stuart Hall with Bill Schwarz, *Familiar Stranger. A Life between Two Islands* (London: Allen Lane, 2017), 194–5; see above, pp. 15–17.

141 https://www.ucl.ac.uk/lbs/ (accessed 09/02/2023).

142 Marcia Langton and Rachel Perkins (eds), *First Australians* (Carlton, Victoria: The Miegunyah Press, 2008), ix–x.

143 https://www.who.com.au/kevin-rudd-sorry-speech (accessed 12/02/2023).

144 Nikole Hannah-Jones, Caitlin Roper, Ilena Silverman and Jake Silverstein (eds), *The 1619 Project* (London: W.H. Allen, 2021), xxii.

145 https://www.politico.com/news/2020/11/02/trump-1776-commission-education-433885 (accessed 09/02/2023).

146 *The Guardian*, 28 April 2018, quoted in Robert Gildea, *Empires of the Mind: The Colonial Past and the Politics of the Present* (Cambridge: Cambridge University Press, 2019), 247.

Chapter 3

1 Jason Steinhauer, *History Disrupted: How Social Media and the World Wide Web have Changed the Past* (Cham: Palgrave Macmillan, 2022).

2 See above, pp. 33–5.

3 Tony Judt, *A History of Europe since 1945* (London: Vintage Books, 2010), 803.

4 See for example Ilan Pappé, *The Ethnic Cleansing of Palestine* (Oxford: Oneworld, 2006).

5 Pierre Seel, *Moi, Pierre Seel, déporté homosexual*. Récit écrit en collaboration avec Jean le Bitoux (Paris: Calmann-Lévy, 1994).

6 https://www.gale.com/intl/c/womens-studies-archive-womens-issues-and-identities (accessed 24/02/2023).

7 https://www.gale.com/intl/c/gay-rights-movement-series-10-lesbian-herstory-archives-newsletter-collection-series-10-lesbian-herstory-archives-newsletter-collection (accessed 24/02/2023).

8 https://www.gale.com/binaries/content/assets/gale-us-en/primary-sources/archives-of-sexuality-and-gender/gct17197880-aca_asg-part-1and2-one-sheet_9_25_17.pdf (accessed 24/02/2023).

9   https://www.whitehouse.gov/briefing-room/speeches-remarks/2022/01/06/remarks-by-president-biden-to-mark-one-year-since-the-january-6th-deadly-assault-on-the-u-s-capitol/ (accessed 23/02/23).

10 https://www.prageru.com/video/was-the-civil-war-about-slavery (accessed 23/02/23).

11 Steinhauer, *History Disrupted*, 1–4.

12 See above, pp. 118–19.

13 Hilary Beckles, *Britain's Black Debt: Reparations for Caribbean Slavery and Native Genocide* (Kingston, Jamaica: University of West Indies Press, 2013); https://caricomreparations.org/ (accessed 23/02/23).

14 Amelia Gentleman, 'Windrush. Home Office has failed to transform its culture, report says', *The Guardian*, 31 Mar. 2022.

15 'They Kept 10,000 Slaves. Now This Family is Paying Up and Saying Sorry', *Observer*, 5 Feb. 2013; Alex Renton, 'Why Can't Britain Talk about Slavery?', *The Guardian*, 11 Feb. 2023; Alex Renton, *Blood Legacy: Reckoning with a Family's Story of Slavery* (Edinburgh: Canongate, 2021); 'Family of PM Gladstone apologise for slavery links', *Observer*, 20 Aug. 2023.

16 See above, pp. 51–2.

17 Charles Devellennes, *The Gilets Jaunes and the New Social Contract* (Bristol: Bristol University Press, 2021).

18 See for example, Robert Gildea, *Backbone of the Nation. Mining Communities and the Great Strike of 1984–85* (New Haven and London: Yale UP, 2023); Florence Sutcliffe-Braithwaite and Natalie Thomlinson, *Women and the Miners' Strike, 1984–85* (Oxford: Oxford University Press, 2023); Jörg Arnold, *The British Miner in the Age of De-industrialization. A Political and Cultural History* (Oxford: Oxford University Press, 2023).

19 Greta Thunberg, *No One is Too Small to Make a Difference* (London: Penguin, 2019), 6–13.

20 Roderick Nash, *Wilderness and the American Mind* [1967] (5th edition, New Haven and London: Yale UP, 2014), 379.

21 Alfred W. Crosby, *The Columbian Exchange: Biological and Cultural Consequences of 1492* (Westport, CT: Greenwood Press, 1972); William Cronon, *Changes in the Land: Indians, Colonists and the Ecology of New England* (New York: Hill and Wang, 1983).

22 David Arnold and Ramachandra Guha (eds), *Nature, Culture, Imperialism. Essays in the Environmental History of South Asia* (Delhi: OUP, 1995).

23 Steinhauer, *History Disrupted*, 87.

24 See for example https://www.timeshighereducation.com/
    campus/collections/decolonising-curriculum; https://www.lgbtq.
    sociology.cam.ac.uk/projects/queer-y-ing-the-curriculum (accessed
    28/02/2023).

25 Claire Alexander, Joya Chatterji and Debbie Weekes-Bernard,
    Making British Histories. Diversity and the National Curriculum
    (London: Runnymede, 2012), 3–14.

26 Alexander, Chatterji and Weekes-Bernard, *History Lessons:
    Teaching Diversity in and through the History National
    Curriculum* (London: Runnymede, 2014), 12.

27 George Ewart Evans, *Ask the Fellows Who Cut the Hay* (London:
    Faber & Faber, 1956).

28 https://www.history.ox.ac.uk/people/dr-priya-atwal (accessed
    30/02/2023).

29 Alex Haley, *Roots* (Garden City, New York: Doubleday, 1976).

30 Stuart Hall with Bill Schwarz, *Familiar Stranger. A Life between
    Two Islands* (London: Allen Lane, 2017), 3, 178, 271.

31 Philippe Sands, *East-West Street: On the Origins of Genocide and
    Crimes against Humanity* (London: Weidenfeld & Nicolson, 2016).

32 Katja Petrowskaja, *Maybe Esther. A Family Story* (London:
    4th Estate, 2018).

33 Vera Brittain, *Testament of Youth* (London: Victor Gollancz, 1933).

34 Carolyn Steedman, *Landscape for a Good Woman: A Story of Two
    Lives* (London: Virago, 1986).

35 Hilda Kean, *London Stories: Personal Lives, Public Histories*
    (London: Rivers Oram Press, 2005).

36 Roy Rozenzweig and David Thelen, 'The Presence of the Past.
    Popular Uses of History in American Life' in Hilda Kean and Paul
    Martin (eds), *The Public History Reader* (London and New York:
    Routledge, 2013), 44–51.

FURTHER READING

General

John H. Arnold, *History: A Very Short Introduction* (Oxford University Press, 2000).

David Cannadine (ed.), *What is History Now?* (Palgrave Macmillan, 2002; 2009).

E.H. Carr, *What is History?* (Penguin, 1964; 1987; 2018).

Helen Carr and Suzannah Lipscomb, *What is History, Now? How the Past and Present Speak to Each Other* (Weidenfeld & Nicolson, 2021).

Margaret MacMillan, *The Uses and Abuses of History* (Profile Books, 2009).

History and myth

Lord Acton, 'Inaugural Lecture on the Study of History' in *Lectures on Modern History* (Macmillan, 1906; Collins, 1960: Bantoche, 2000), or in *Essays on Freedom and Power* (Thames and Hudson, 1956).

Nigel Biggar, *Colonialism: A Moral Reckoning* (William Collins, 2023).

Angus Calder, *The Myth of the Blitz* (Jonathan Cape, 1991).

Caroline Elkins, *Legacy of Violence: A History of the British Empire* (Bodley Head, 2022).

Moses Finley, 'Myth, Memory and History' in Finley, *The Use and Abuse of History* (Pimlico, 1975; 1990; 2000), pp. 11–33.

Eric Hobsbawm and Terence Ranger (eds), *The Invention of Tradition* (Cambridge University Press, 1983).

Saburō Ienaga, *Japan's Last War: World War II and the Japanese* (Blackwell, 1979).

Henrietta Marshall, *Our Island Story: A History of Britain for Boys and Girls* [1905] (new edition, Phoenix, 2010; 2014).

Peter Novick, *That Noble Dream: The 'Objectivity Question' and the American Historical Profession* (Cambridge University Press, 1988).

Raphael Samuel and Paul Thompson (eds), *The Myths We Live By* (Routledge, 1990).

History and power

Edmund Burke, *Reflections on the Revolution in France* [1790] (Pelican Books, 1968; 1986; 2004).

François Furet, *Interpreting the French Revolution* (Cambridge University Press, 1981).

Christopher Hill, 'The Norman Yoke', in Hill, *Puritanism and Revolution: Studies in the Interpretation of the English Revolution in the 17th Century* (Secker and Warburg, 1958), pp. 50–122.

Abraham Lincoln, *The Gettysburg Address* [1863] (Penguin, 2009).

Roderick MacFarquhar and Michael Schoenhals, *Mao's Last Revolution* (Belknap Press of Harvard University Press, 2006).

Karl Marx and Friedrich Engels, *The Communist Manifesto* [1848], ed. Gareth Stedman Jones (Penguin, 2002).

Thomas Paine, *The Rights of Man* [1791–2] (Penguin Books, 1969; 1985).

M.N.S. Sellers, *American Republicanism, Roman Ideology and the United States Constitution* (Macmillan, 1994).

Leon Trotsky, *The Revolution Betrayed: What is the Soviet Union and Where is it Going?* [1936] (Dover Publications, 2004).

History and identity

Raewyn Connell, *Masculinities* (Polity, 1995, 2005).

Heather Cox Richardson, *How the South Won the Civil War: Oligarchy, Democracy, and the Continuing Fight for the Soul of America* (Oxford University Press, 2020).

William Cronon, *Changes in the Land: Indians, Colonists and the Ecology of New England* (Hill and Wang, 1983).

W.E.B. Du Bois, 'The Souls of the White Folk' [1910], in Du Bois, *Darkwater: Voices from within the Veil* (Verso, 2016), pp. 17–29

Eric Foner, *Who Owns History? Rethinking the Past in a Changing World* (Hill and Wang, 2002).

Priyamvada Gopal, *Insurgent Empire: Anticolonial Resistance and British Dissent* (Verso, 2019).

Stuart Hall with Bill Schwarz, *Familiar Stranger: A Life between Two Islands* (Allen Lane, 2017).

Nikole Hannah-Jones, Caitlin Roper, Ilena Silverman and Jake Silverstein (eds), *The 1619 Project* (W.H. Allen, 2021).

Ibram X. Kendi, *Stamped from the Beginning: The Definitive History of Racist Ideas in America* (Nation Books, 2016).

Juliet Mitchell, *Women: The Longest Revolution – Essays on Feminism, Literature and Psychoanalysis* (Virago, 1984).

Gary B. Nash, Charlotte Crabtree and Ross E. Dunn, *History on Trial. The Culture Wars and the Teaching of the Past* (Vintage Books, 2000).

David Olusoga, *Black and British: A Forgotten History* (Macmillan, 2016).

Henry Reynolds, *An Indelible Stain? The Question of Genocide in Australia's History* (Viking, 2001).

Edward Said, *Orientalism: Western Conceptions of the Orient* (Penguin, 1995).

Susan Stryker, *Transgender History. The Roots of Today's Revolution* (2nd edn., Seal Press, 2017).

E.P. Thompson, *The Making of the English Working Class* (Penguin, 1968; 2013).

Joan Wallach Scott, 'Gender: a useful category of historical analysis', *American Historical Review* 91(5) (1986).

Doing history

Lynn Abrams, *Oral History Theory* (Routledge, 2010; 2016).

Anthony Adolph, *Tracing your Family History* (Collins, 2004; 2007).

Claire Alexander, Joya Chatterji and Debbie Weekes-Bernard, *Making British Histories: Diversity and the National Curriculum* (Runnymede, 2012).

Hilda Kean, *London Stories: Personal Lives, Public Histories* (Rivers Oram Press, 2005).

Sheila Rowbotham, *Promise of a Dream: Remembering the Sixties* (Penguin, 2000).

Jason Steinhauer, *History Disrupted: How Social Media and the World Wide Web have Changed the Past* (Palgrave Macmillan, 2022).

INDEX

References to figures appear in *italic* type;
those in **bold** type refer to boxes.

A

Aboriginal history 112–13,
116–18
Adams, Herbert Baxter 38
Alexander, Claire 134–5
Alexander III of Russia 80
Algeria 30
American Civil War 13, 68–71,
73, 126
American independence 12, 61–3,
62
Amritsar massacre 30
Anderson, Benedict 42
Anderson, David 51
Anglo-Saxons 33, 36–7
Anti-Islamism 50, 51–2
Apess, William 111
Armenian genocide 29
Arnold, David 132
Aron, Robert 43
Atwal, Priya 136
Augustus Caesar 57
Austen, Jane 100

B

Bancroft, Hubert Howe 38
Banner, Lois 104
Barruel, Abbé Augustin 65–6
Beard, Charles and Mary 69–70
Beauvoir, Simone de 102–3
Bebel, August 92–3

Beckles, Hilary 128
Benson, Arthur 25
Biden, Joe 2–4, 17, 125–6
Biggar, Nigel 16–17, 52, 53
Black history 110–12, 113–17,
118–20, 136–7
Black Lives Matter 13, *127*
Bouteflika, Abdelaziz 30
Bowers, Claude 71
British Empire 13–17, 26, 28, 30,
37, 47, 48, 50, 51, 52–3, 116
British monarchy 9–11, 32–3,
56–7, 59–61, 67
Brittain, Vera 138
Broyelle, Jacques and Claudie 85
Bruce Gilley 52
Bryant, Arthur **10**, 40, 41
Brzezinski, Zbigniew 76–7
Burke, Edmund 64–5
Bury, J.B. 39
Butler, Judith 108
Butterfield, Herbert **37**, 41–2
Byzantine Empire 20–1

C

Camus, Renaud 51–2
Canada, residential schools 117
Cannadine, David 11
Carr, E.H. 55, 76
Certeau, Michel de 100
Chaadayev, Peter 7

Chamberlin, William 75
Charlemagne, King of the Franks 20
Charles I, British King 59, 60, 61, 77, 78
Charles III, British King 10
Chartist movement 90–1, 100
Chatterji, Joya 134–5
Chiang Kai-shek 82
China 8–9, 12, 28, 55–6, 80–7
Churchill, Winston 10, 41, 43
Cicero 31
civil rights movement 71–3, 115
Clare, Anthony 109
Clarendon, Lord 78
Coke, Sir Edward 59
Cole, Douglas (G.D.H.) 96
colonialism 13–17, 24–6, 29–30, 47–51, 52–3, 116–17, 128–9
Colston, Edward 13–14
Commager, Henry Steele 114
community history 134–6
Conquest, Robert 77
Cooper, Anna Julia 111
Cox, Karen 73
Cronon, William 132
Crosby, Alfred 132
Cultural Revolution (China) 82–6, **84**, *85*
Czech nationalism 23

D
Darlan, Admiral François 107
Davis, Jefferson 13, 68–9
Declaration of Independence (US) 61, *62*, 68–9, 71
Declaration of the Rights of Man (France) 64, 97–8
Deng Xiaoping 81, 83
Douglass, Frederick 111
Du Bois, W.E.B. 25–6
Duby, Georges 106

E
Egyptian mythology 19
e-history 122
1848 revolutions 66–7, 105
Eisenstein, Sergei 28, 76
Elgar, Edward 25
Elizabeth II, British Queen 9–10
Elkins, Caroline 51, 53
Engels, Friedrich 90, 101–2
English Civil War 59–60, 77–8
English Commonwealth 59–61
environmental history 130–2
Evans, George Ewart 135–6
Extinction Rebellion (XR) 131, 132

F
family history 136–9
Fanon, Frantz 47
feminist history 100–10, 124–5
Ferguson, Niall 50
Ferré, Théophile 91
Ferry, Jules 25
Finberg, Leslie 109
First World War 26–7, 45
Fischer, Fritz 45
Flexner, Eleanor 103
Floyd, George 13
Foner, Eric 72–3
France 21, 23–4, 26–7, 28, 30, 38–9, 43–4, 51–2, 63–6, 67–8, 73–4, 78–80, 85, 91, 97–8, 99–100, 105–6, 124, 130
Freeman, Edward Augustus 36
Friedan, Betty 103
Furet, François 79–80

G
Gallagher, Gary 73
Gallagher, John 47
Gast, John 25
Gellner, Ernest 42

gender history 104, 106–10, 124–5
Geoffrey of Monmouth 32–3
George III, British King 61
Germany 26–7, 29–30, 32, 34–5, 39, 41, 45–6, 92–3, 98–9, 100, 123–4
Gettysburg Address 69
Geyl, Pieter 88
gilets jaunes movement 130
Gladstone, John 128
Goldman, Emma 106
Gompers, Samuel 93–4
Gopal, Priyamvada 52
Gorbachev, Mikhail 78, 83
Gove, Michael 9
Great Replacement Theory 51–2, 128–9
Greece 19, 31–2
Guha, Ramachandra 132
Guha, Ranajit 48

H
Habermas, Jürgen 46
Haley, Alex 136
Hall, Catherine 16, 116, 137
Hall, Stuart 115–16, 136–7
Hamilton, Alexander 62–3
Hammond, Lawrence and Barbara 96
Hannah-Jones, Nikole 118
Hanotaux, Gabriel 39
Hawthorne, Julian 38
Herder, Johann Gottfried 21–2
Herodotus 19, 31
Heywood, Linda 115
Hill, Christopher 77–8, 97
Hinton, William 83
historical frames 49
historical novels 33, 34
'History Lessons' project 134–5
History Workshop movement 99–100

Hitler, Adolf 27
Hobsbawm, Eric 42, 97, 99
Holocaust 29, 123–4, 125, 137
Holy Roman Empire 20, 21
Homer 19, 31
Howard, John 118
Hung Hsiu-ch'uan 81
Huntington, Samuel 50
Hus, Jan 23
Hyde, Edward 60

I
Ienaga, Saburō 46
India 30, 48
Indigenous history 110–11, 112–13, 116–20, 132
Italian nationalism 23
Ivan the Terrible 76

J
Jackson, Andrew 13
James VI/I, British King 59
Japan 28, 41, 46
Jaurès, Jean 97–8
Jeffrey, Sheila 107
Jewish history 27, 29, 35, 43, 123–4, 137
Johnson, Boris 15
Johnson, Linton Kwesi 120
Jones, Claudia 112
Judt, Tony 124
Julius Caesar 12, 57, 58

K
Kay-Shuttleworth, James 90
Kean, Hilda 138
Keppler, Udo 25, 26
King, Martin Luther 71
Kipling, Rudyard 26
Kocka, Jürgen 98
Kohl, Helmut 45
Krafft, Johann Peter 22

L
labour history 90–100, 129–30
Labrousse, Ernest 98, 105
Langlois, Charles-Victor 38
Langton, Marcia 116
language 21–2, 23
Last Night of the Proms 14–15
Lavisse, Ernest 39
Le Bitoux, Jean 107, 125
Le Pen, Marine 51
Lenin, Vladimir 74–5, 78, 80
Leopold II, King of Belgium 13
Levellers 59
Lévy-Willard, Annette 106
Lewis, Bernard 50
LGBTQ+ history 104, 106–10,
   124–5
Lincoln, Abraham 68, 69
Lissagaray, Prosper-Olivier 91
Livy (Titus Livius) 57
Lovett, William 91
Lüdtke, Alf 100
Lukács, György 34

M
Macaulay, Catharine 60–1
Macaulay, Thomas Babington 67
Machiavelli, Niccolò 57–8
MacMillan, Margaret 22
Magna Carta 59
Maitron, Jean 98
Malik, Kenan 129
Mandate of Heaven (China)
   55–6, 80, 81
Manifest Destiny (US) 24–5, 38
Mao Zedong 81–3, **84**
Mariángela 10
Marshall, Henrietta Elizabeth **10**
Martov, Julius 74
Marx, Eleanor 91
Marx, Karl 67–8, 74, 90
Marxist history 77–8, **79**, 96–7,
   99

masculinity 108–9
Mau Mau 30
Mazzini, Giuseppe 23
Medvedev, Roy 77
Merrie England 39–40, **40**
#MeToo movement 125
Michel, Louise 91, 100–1
Michelet, Jules 66
Mickiewicz, Adam 23
Milton, John 60
Mirza, Heidi Safia 108
Mitchell, Juliet 103
monarchical power 54, 56–7,
   58–9
Montesquieu 62–3
Morison, Samuel Eliot 114

N
Namibia 29–30
Napoleon I 21, 66, 73, 86, 88
Napoleon III 74
Nash, Roderick 132
nationalism 21–4, 22, 42
Native American history 13,
   24–5, 88, 111
Nazi Germany 27, 45–6, 125
Nolte, Ernst 46
Norman Yoke doctrine 59
Nwanoku, Chi-chi 15

O
Olusoga, David 16
Orthodox Christian Church 20, 21
Orwell, George 12–13, 54
O'Sullivan, John L. 24–5
Ottoman Turks 20–1, 23

P
Paine, Tom 65
Palacký, František 23
Pankhurst, Emmeline 101
Paris Commune 74–5, 82, 91, **92**,
   93, **93**, 105

Paxton, Robert 43
Perkins, Charles (Charlie) 113
Perkins, Rachel 117
Perrot, Michelle 98, 105–6
Petrowskaja, Katja 137
Phillips, Ulrich Bonnell 70–1
Picq, Françoise 106
podcasts 133
Poland 3, 23
Ponting, Clive 42–3
postcolonial history 47–9, **49**, 52–3, 128–9
Postgate, Margaret and Raymond 96
Pozhigailo, Pavel 7
Prussia 23, 35
public history 135–9
Putin, Vladimir 1–7, 5, 7, 80

Q
queer history 104, 106–10, 124–5

R
Randall, J.G. 71
Ranger, Terence 42
Ranke, Leopold von 33–5, 123, 139
Raspail, Jean 51
Reagan, Ronald 45, 119
Reed, John 75
Renan, Ernest 23–4, 38–9
Rendall, Jane 105
Renton, Alex 128
republican model 54, 57–8, 59–66
Restoration 60
revisionism **44**
revolutions 12, 54–5, 73–5, 78–83, 97–8
Reynolds, David 43
Rhodes, Cecil 14
Ritter, Gerhard 45

Roberts, Andrew 51
Robespierre, Maximilien 64, 73
Robinson, Joan 83
Robinson, Ronald 47
Roman empire 19–20, 31, 32, 57, *58*
Roof, Dylann 126
Roper, Michael 108
Rossi, Alice 104
Rousso, Henry 43
Rowbotham, Sheila 105, 106
Rowse, A.L. **10**, 40, 41
Rudd, Kevin 118
'Rule Britannia' 14–15
Russia 1–7, *5*, 7, 8, 12, 20–1, 28–9, 74–80
Rwanda 29

S
Said, Edward 47–8
Saint-Just, Louis de 63–4
Samuel, Raphael 97, 99
Sands, Philippe 137
sati 48
Satia, Priya 52–3
Schafer, Boyd C. 42
Schoenhals, Michael 86
Schram, Stuart 83
scientific history 33–5, **34**
Scott, Joan Wallach 107–8
Scott, Sir Walter 33, 34, **34**, 36
Sécher, Reynald 78–9
Second World War 28–9, 41, 42–6
Seeley, J.R. 36, 37
Seidule, Ty 126, 133
Seignobos, Charles 38
Shaw, George Bernard 53
Shevchenko, Taras 23
Sitkof, Harvard 115
slavery 13–17, 68–73, 70, 72, 110, 111, 114–15, 116, 118–19, 120, 125–8

Smith, Arthur Lee 115
Snyder, Timothy 5–6
Soboul, Albert 98
Sorel, Albert 39
Speer, Albert 27
Spivak, Gayatri Chakravorty
    48
Stafford, Edmund 56–7
Stalin, Joseph 6, 7, 75–7, 80
Stampp, Kenneth 72
statues 5, 13–14, **14**
Stedman Jones, Gareth 100
Steedman, Carolyn 138
Stock, Kathleen 100
Stolypin, Pyotr 80
Stonewall Riots 107
Stryker, Susan 109
Stubbs, William 36
subaltern studies 48
suffragettes 101, *102*, 103
Sun Yat-sen 81

T
Tacitus 32, 35
Taylor Greene, Marjorie 17
Tharoor, Shashi 52
Thiers, Adolphe 66
Thompson, E.B. 97
Thorne, Will 94
Thucydides 31–2
Thunberg, Greta 131
Thurston, Anne 85–6
Tiananmen Square 9, 83–4
Todd, Selina 100
Tosh, John 108
trade unions 94, 95, 96, 99, 130
Treitschke, Heinrich von 35
Trevelyan, George Macaulay
    39–40
Trevelyan, Laura 128
Trevor-Roper, Hugh 77–8, 110
Trojan war 19, 31
Trotsky, Leon 75–6

Trump, Donald 6, 17, 119–20
Turner, Frederick Jackson 38
Turner, Sharon 36

U
Ukraine 1–6, 23
United States 2–4, 6, 12, 13, 17,
    24–6, 38, 50, 61–3, 62, 68–73,
    93–4, 103, 104, 107, 111–12,
    114–15, 118–20, 125–7, *127*

V
Vichy regime 28, 43, 107
Victoria, British Queen 11
Virgil 19–20
Vladimir the Great 5, *5*

W
Walker, Shaun 4, 5
Wang Dong 81
Webb, Sidney and Beatrice 95–6
Wedgwood, Veronica 78
Weeks, Jeffrey 107
Wehler, Hans-Ulrich 98
Whig history **10**, 36, **37**, 77–8
William and Mary (British King
    and Queen) 67
Williams, Wendy 128
Windrush generation 112, 120,
    128
Wittig, Monique 106–7
women's history 48, 100–10,
    111, 124–5, 129–30
Woodson, Carter Godwin 113–14
working class history 90–100,
    129–30

X
Xi Jinping 8–9, 86–7

Z
Zheng Yi 86
Zinn, Howard 115